"One of the most vital partners for schools and families working towards the educational success and wellness of youth is community-based organizations, as compellingly illustrated in this important book by Anjela Wong. *Opening Doors* looks deeply at one such organization, follows several Chinese American immigrant youth and families as they navigate institutional and social contexts, and reveals not only the support that is needed out of schools but also the frameworks from advocacy that can improve educational policy and practice. At a time when immigration rhetoric and reform is front and center, let's all read and discuss this book."

—Kevin Kumashiro, author of *Bad Teacher!: How Blaming Teachers Distorts the Bigger Picture*

Opening Doors

sj Miller & Leslie David Burns
GENERAL EDITORS

Vol. 7

The Social Justice Across Contexts in Education series is
part of the Peter Lang Education list.
Every volume is peer reviewed and meets
the highest quality standards for content and production.

PETER LANG
New York • Bern • Frankfurt • Berlin
Brussels • Vienna • Oxford • Warsaw

Nga-Wing Anjela Wong

Opening Doors

Community Centers Connecting Working-Class Immigrant Families and Schools

PETER LANG
New York • Bern • Frankfurt • Berlin
Brussels • Vienna • Oxford • Warsaw

Library of Congress Cataloging-in-Publication Data

Names: Wong, Nga-Wing Anjela, author.
Title: Opening doors: community centers connecting working-class
immigrant families and schools / Nga-Wing Anjela Wong.
Description: New York: Peter Lang, 2018.
Series: Social justice across contexts in education, vol. 7
ISSN 2372-6849 (print) | ISSN 2372-6857 (online)
Includes bibliographical references and index.
Identifiers: LCCN 2017028865 | ISBN 978-1-4331-4685-5 (hardback: alk. paper)
ISBN 978-1-4331-4686-2 (pbk: alk. paper) | ISBN 978-1-4331-4687-9 (ebook pdf)
ISBN 978-1-4331-4688-6 (epub) | ISBN 978-1-4331-4689-3 (mobi)
Subjects: LCSH: Community centers—United States.
Social work with Youth—United States. | Asian Americans—Education—United States.
Asian Americans—Cultural assimilation. | Youth centers—United States.
Immigrant children—Education—United States.
Community and School—United States.
Education—Parent participation—United States.
Classification: LCC HN43 .W66 2018 | DDC 362.70973—dc23
LC record available at https://lccn.loc.gov/2017028865
DOI 10.3726/b11595

Bibliographic information published by **Die Deutsche Nationalbibliothek**.
Die Deutsche Nationalbibliothek lists this publication in the "Deutsche
Nationalbibliografie"; detailed bibliographic data are available
on the Internet at http://dnb.d-nb.de/.

To
my family,
my community, and
all the youth and elders who have fought and
continue to fight against oppression!

Table of contents

Acknowledgments

I am deeply grateful to many people for supporting me with this project.

First and foremost, I would like to thank my mommie and baba, Hoi Yan and Wing Yiu Wong, who have been a constant source of love, encouragement, and inspiration to me. Their resiliency offered me a place and space to pursue my dreams and persevere in life while keeping me grounded, humble, and honest. My lovin' brothers, Alex and Alden Wong, have kept me sane with much laughs, love, and AAA memories! My paternal grandparents (yau yau and ngeen ngeen), Wong Ping Tsek and Yu Choi Kay, as well as goo ma Enid Wong, sok por Lau Fung Kun, Shelley Yee, my maternal grandparents, the entire Lau, Wong, Yee, and Yu familia, as well as my ancestors and elders have paved the way and laid the foundations for future generations.

Gloria Ladson-Billings (my Ph.D. advisor), Stacey Lee (my master's advisor), and Lynet Uttal: Much gratitude for always giving me so much time and feedback and providing me a space to strengthen my ideas, voice, and research. It is a tremendous honor to be able to work with such distinguished scholars who are teaching much needed classes and engaging in extremely important research. Your encouraging words and support made me belong in academia. I will always remember our dialogues where your encouraging words, advocacy, and guidance were truly appreciated!

I wish to thank sj Miller, Sarah Bode, Les Burns, Tim Swenarton, Sara McBride, and Luke McCord for their positive energy and gratitude throughout the entire process and all of the extraordinary staff at Peter Lang whose work pre-, in, and postproduction made this book possible, including the anonymous reviewers whose encouragement and suggestions strengthened this book. Thanks to sj Miller whose commitment and patience to this book have been invaluable.

To all of my educators, professors, and mentors that I had the opportunity to take courses with and/or learn from throughout my academic journey: Michael Apple, Wayne Au, Joanne Barker, Grace Lee Boggs, Bryan Brayboy, Patricia Burch, Jeff Chan, Malcolm Collier, Júlio Diniz-Pereira, Lorraine Dong, Thea Renda Abu El-Haj, Ms. Eng, Michael Fultz, Robert Fung, Mary Louise Gomez, Dan Gonzales, Marlon Hom, Brad Hughes and the WC staff, Shirley Hune, Madeline Hsu, Donna Hubbard, Peter Kiang, Nancy Kendall, Madhulika Khandelwal, Ben Kobashigawa, Yuri Kochiyama, Gloria Ladson-Billings, Stacey Lee, Ms. Leung, Dawn Mabalon, Eric Mar, Trinh Nguyen, Michael Olneck, Dan Pekarsky, Clarissa Rojas, Simone Schweber, Ms. Shee, Lai Lai Sheung, Rajini Srikanth, Betty Szeto, Minh Hoa Ta, Ate Allyson Tintiango-Cubales, Thầy Trần Bắc, Patrick Tran, Dorothy Tsurata, Phany Tum, Lynet Uttal, Angela Valenzuela, Benito Sunny Vergara, Craig Werner, Diane Williams, Linda Wing, Bernard Wong, Vivian Wu, Yeung bak bak, Grace Yoo, Zheng Xin-Rong, the University of Wisconsin-Madison's School of Education—particularly the Department of Educational Policy Studies, San Francisco State University's College of Ethnic Studies, Department of Asian American Studies, SFSU's 2002 AAS graduate students—Japheth Aquino, Tracy Buenavista, Kelly Vaughn, and Jeannie Wu), and the 1968 Third World Liberation Front!

I have been fortunate to connect with fabulous people through the years over delicious food, critical dialogues, outdoor adventures, and/or joyous laughter: Vonzell Agosto, the Anand and Christiansen familia (Ari, Rachel, Gita, and Vayu), the Au and Shimabukuro familia (Mira, Wayne, and Makoto), Anita Bergevin, Bethany Brent, Karen Bretz, Anthony Brown, Keffrelyn Brown, Lolly Carpluk, Angelina Castagno, Gary Chan, Minerva Chavez, Jian Bo Chen, Prisca Chinn and the Chinn familia, Hoewook Chung, Taína Collazo-Quiles, Júlio Diniz-Pereira, Jason Erdmann, Marni Finch, Eugene Fujimoto, Mariecris Gatlabayan, Mary Jo Gessler, Suzanne Hancock, Tommy Hancock, Richie Heard, Maureen Hogan, Jenee Jerome, Manjula Joseph, Andreas Kazamias, Kyoko Kishimoto, Thomas Ku, Kevin Kumashiro, Doug Larkin, Anpu Lau, Cindy Lau, Maggie Lee, Beth Leonard, Mike Leonard, Andrea, Mariann and Bob Litznerski, Elaine Liu, Christine Marasigan, Tori Maslow, Caitlin Montague, Heather Ann Moody, Cindy Mui, Gilbert Park, Lirio Patton, Oiyan Poon, Stace Rierson, Ricardo Kiko

Rosa, Victoria Rosin, Darlene St. Clair, Lilliana Patricia Saldaña, David Shih, Olga Skinner, Marian Slaughter, Lotchanna Sourivong, Brenda Spychalla, Phitsamay Sychitkokhong, True Thao, Ate Allyson Tintiango-Cubales, Kabzuag Vaj, Meng Vaj, Virginia Waddick, Sophia Ward, Adriane Williams, Gloria Williams, Maria Williams, Arthur and Maggie Yang, Gloria Grad Group, Stacey Grad Group, the Coalition for Asian Pacific American Youth (CAPAY), Pin@y Educational Partnerships (PEP)—particularly PEP Balboa 2001–2002, SFSU Asian Student Union, Freedom, Inc. and the Asian Freedom Project, UW-Madison EPS 200 fall 2006 and EPS FIG fall 2005, UMass Boston's Institute for Asian American Studies (Paul Watanabe, Michael Liu, and Shauna Lo), 2009–2010 SCSU Hmong Student Organization, UWEC Hmong Student Association (shout outs to the 2014–2015, 2015–2016, 2016–2017 EBoards), UAF graduate advisees, and my extraordinarily brilliant UWEC student-faculty research team (Ameririta Chhunn, Yer Lor, Jackson Yang, and Pang Kou Yang). My graduate assistants provided much needed support. Cheyenne Braker and Kayla Van Allen tracked down citations. My amazing students—thank you for allowing me to teach *and* learn from you. Wayne Au, Tommy Hancock, Suzanne Hancock, Beth Leonard, Lilliana Patricia Saldaña, Mira Shimabukuro, and Mommie, Baba, Alex, and Alden Wong will always hold a very special place in my heart. They energized the research and (re) writing process for me when I needed it the most.

Most importantly, I thank my research collaborators (the young people, their parents, and HCCC staff) for taking the time to share their stories (the struggles and, more importantly, the survivals!) as well as for inspiring me each and every day to effect positive change on Mother Earth. Be roses that grow in concrete.

peace & love

*****

Foreword

WAYNE AU

I write this foreword in dismal times for immigrants in the United States. As has been too often the case in the history of the United States, anti-immigrant rhetoric, anti-immigrant policies, and anti-immigrant violence have once again returned with disturbing potency. African, Latinx, Muslim, and Asian immigrant families in the United States are operating with increased fear of not just attacks from White supremacists, but also community raids by ICE—both of which have been emboldened through the xenophobic, anti-immigrant policies advanced by the administration of U.S. President Donald Trump. In the midst of this, teachers report that they have children crying in their classrooms, as these immigrant students worry about their own families and communities (Au, 2017).

I paint this dreary picture not to depress, but rather to be crystal clear about the realities facing our children of immigrant students. As Nga-Wing Anjela Wong reminds us so astutely in *Opening Doors: Community Centers Connecting Working-Class Immigrant Families and Schools*, between home, school, and community, children of immigrants traverse multiple worlds every day of their lives, with each world presenting both unique stresses and unique resources as they make their ways. The stories here, in the voices of the young people themselves, tell us that, if we are going to serve our children of immigrant students well, then we need to make sure that they have access to a multitude of resources—including access to flourishing networks of community-based organizations (CBOs).

What I find most important in Wong's *Opening Doors* is that it calls us to commit to *community* in education in very fundamental and profound ways. For instance, *Opening Doors* reinforces the reality that out-of-school time is critical in the educational success of students. We have known this from decades of research showing that nonschool factors influence educational achievement far more than in-school factors (Berliner, 2013). What Wong offers us is insight into how a material, nonschool community resource, in this case the Harborview Chinatown Community Center (HCCC), concretely contributes to working class students from Chinese immigrant families to navigate the U.S. school system.

Another way that *Opening Doors* shows us the power of committing to community in education is through the level of community groundedness of the HCCC generally, and the Community Youth Center (CYC) program specifically. Both the HCCC and the CYC are not only geographically located in Harborview's Chinese immigrant community, but they are also culturally and linguistically located in that community. This is a lesson in effectiveness, where culturally relevant (Ladson-Billings, 1995) pedagogy and curriculum is paramount to the HCCC's success in reaching the Chinese American youth and their families who access the services there.

Commitment to community also shines through *Opening Doors* in how Wong honors what resources exist within the Chinese immigrant community itself. The HCCC and CYC represent education *for* the community, *by* the community, and in doing so they illustrate the kinds of community cultural wealth (Yosso, 2005) and funds of knowledge (Moll, Amanti, Neff, & Gonzalez, 1992) that exist among the Chinese immigrant families there. This point is especially important because it shows how, by providing institutional structure and amplification of community knowledge, CBOs like the HCCC can help equalize the differences in power between immigrant communities and schools—in this case essentially providing Chinese immigrants with their own institution to help them contend with other institutions outside of their community, like school.

Further, in being so grounded in community—and in such loving and caring ways, I might add—Wong's book paints a complex and living portrait of the Harborview Chinese American immigrant students. What happens in the process is something beautiful, as the students' own voices give *Opening Doors* the power to destroy stereotypes about Asian American students generally, and Chinese American students specifically, being "model minorities." So instead of the stereotype, Wong once again reminds us that in reality, like other working class children of Asian immigrants in the United States (Lee & Kumashiro, 2005; Lew, 2006), the Chinese American immigrant students in *Opening Doors* are not magical Asian academic juggernauts. Rather, they need the support and community resources provided by the HCCC to be successful in schools.

For all these reasons, *Opening Doors: Community Centers Connecting Working-Class Immigrant Families and Schools* is an important contribution to the scholarship on immigrant education, as well as that of Asian American education. It breathes life into the experiences of working class, Chinese American immigrant students, and in the process shows all of us that we have a lot to learn from CBOs and their models of grounded, culturally relevant education. Perhaps most important, Wong's work demonstrates how, in these times of hypernationalist, White racism, we need to be fighting for resources for our immigrant students.

Wayne Au
Professor, School of Educational Studies
University of Washington, Bothell
Editor, *Rethinking Schools*

Works cited

Au, W. (2017). When multicultural education is not enough. *Multicultural Perspectives, 19*(3), 1–4. doi:10.1080/15210960.2017.1331741

Berliner, D. C. (2013). Effects of inequality and poverty vs. teachers and schooling on America's youth. *Teachers College Record, 115*(12). Retrieved from http://www.tcrecord.org

Ladson-Billings, G. (1995). Toward a theory of culturally relevant pedagogy. *American Educational Research Journal, 32*(3), 465–491.

Lee, S. J., & Kumashiro, K. (2005). *A report on the status of Asian Americans and Pacific Islanders in education: Beyond the "model minority" stereotype* (p. 32). Washington, DC: National Education Association.

Lew, J. (2006). *Asian Americans in class: Charting the achievement gap among Korean American youth.* New York, NY: Teachers College Press.

Moll, L. C., Amanti, C., Neff, D., & Gonzalez, N. (1992). Funds of knowledge for teaching: Using a qualitative approach to connect homes and classrooms. *Theory into Practice, 31*(2), 132–141. doi:10.1080/00405849209543534

Yosso, T. J. (2005). Whose culture has capital? A critical race theory discussion of community cultural wealth. *Race Ethnicity and Education, 8*(1), 69–91. doi:10.1080/1361332052000341006

Abbreviations

AAPI: Asian Americans and Pacific Islanders
ASP: Afterschool program
CBO: Community-based organization
CDP: Chinatown Development Plan
OST: Out-of-school time

CHAPTER ONE

Community-based organizations centering family-community-school partnerships

Michelle came to the United States in 2003 at the age of ten with her mom and younger brother from Toisan, China. After being separated from her dad for five years, the family was finally reunited. Michelle's dad worked as a chef in Toisan and after he arrived in the United States, he continued as a chef at a small Chinese restaurant. Similar to all of the youth in this research, Michelle and her family came through the family reunification preference under the 1965 Immigration and Naturalization Act. Her father immigrated to the United States five years prior in 1998 when his parents, who have been in the United States for more than ten years, sponsored him. Michelle described how at first she was "very shy when I saw my dad because I haven't seen him for such a long time." However, once they started talking and spending time together their relationship grew closer. Michelle remembers her father taking them around the city for the first two months and "sitting by the harbor and watching boats pass by because my little brother loves boats." Shortly after Michelle arrived, her dad saw "a flier on the street" that the Harborview Chinatown Community Center (HCCC) offered English classes and enrichment programs for adults, youth, and children. This was Michelle's first introduction to HCCC and its youth program, the Community Youth Center (CYC). HCCC, the largest Asian American social service provider in the state, is an ethnic multiservice 501(c)(3) nonprofit organization that began in the late 1960s as a grassroots community effort.

Similar to other recent immigrants, Michelle and her family lived with relatives for the first few months. Later, they moved into a two-bedroom rental apartment that was upstairs of a local Chinese grocery store in Chinatown. In order to cover the $1,000 plus rent and other expenses, Michelle's dad had to work extra hours, which resulted in limited family interactions. Moreover, Michelle's mother immediately started looking for work because the cost of living was "just extremely high." Through the help of family members, her mom found temporary assembly-line work, such as "putting papers together and peeling crabs."

Five months after the family was reunited, Michelle's father was diagnosed with liver cancer. During the treatment stage, her father continued to work because "the rent was really expensive." A few months later, her father passed away. During this time Michelle, who was only eleven, felt "extremely unhappy and unlucky." After the death of their father, the family moved downstairs to a one-bedroom apartment because they could not afford the two-bedroom apartment. Instead of paying over $1,000 for a two-bedroom apartment, rent was now $685 per month. Michelle's family structure immediately shifted after her father's death.

Michelle's mother was enrolled in the Adult English class at HCCC and around that time a family friend, who was from the same village, referred her to a seamstress opening at a garment factory. Since her mother was working and taking English classes, Michelle was responsible for taking her younger brother to their grandparents' apartment in the mornings to catch the school bus before she went to school and then picking him up around 6 p.m. from the afterschool program (ASP). This gave Michelle added responsibility, especially being a youth, a recent immigrant, and living in a single parent household. I remember on several occasions while at CYC we were either singing karaoke or playing ping-pong or games, and Michelle had to leave in the middle to pick up her brother. Occasionally, Michelle would also need to cook dinner if her mother worked overtime at the garment factory. At the age of ten, Michelle served as a bridge for her mom with the outside world. I recall during one of our interviews in 2005 I asked Michelle how she could remember all the dates so vividly (e.g., immigration dates, parents' occupation start and end dates, housing applications, etc.). She said with a smile, "because I help my mom fill out application forms all the time." Initially, Michelle came to CYC because of its English classes, and then gradually, with the encouragements from her friends and the staffs, she began to take part in various CYC's programs throughout her middle and high school years.

Michelle's narrative broadly illustrates (1) the immigration experience of the many 1st (i.e., those who came to the United States after the age of 12) and 1.5 generation (i.e., those who came to the United States before the age of 12) youth in this research, (2) the responsibilities and roles children of immigrants play for their family, and (3) how they heard about and got involved with HCCC and CYC. The term "children of immigrants" refers to both U.S.-born (i.e., second generation) and foreign-born (i.e., the first and 1.5 generation) children and while there are differences in their experiences, "they nevertheless share an important common denominator: immigrant parents" (Suárez-Orozco & Suárez-Orozco, 2001, p. 1). All of the youth in this research were introduced to HCCC and CYC through their ethnic and social networks, such as family members, friends, parent's friends, schoolteachers, or community workers (Lew, 2003; Louie, 2004; Zhou & Bankston, 1998). The reciprocal process continues where they tell and recruit their friend and family networks because, as I will illustrate, "CYC is my home and family."

Children of immigrants are the fastest growing population in the United States; therefore addressing their needs has become an important issue facing educators, researchers, and policy makers nationwide. Additionally, Asian Americans are the fastest growing racial group in the United States. More importantly, working-poor and low-income immigrant families of color need support and resources to be able to negotiate and navigate between their home/community and their school/dominant society (Lee, 2005; Lew, 2006; Pang, Kiang, & Pak, 2004). Educational research on post-1965 children of immigrants has highlighted the special challenges that these young people face as they negotiate between two "worlds": their home/community culture and school/dominant culture (Gibson, 1988; Lee, 2001, 2005; Li, 2003; Lopez, 2003; Olsen, 1997; Phelan, Davidson, & Yu, 1998; Stanton-Salazar, 2001; Suárez-Orozco & Suárez-Orozco, 2001; Valdés, 1996, 2001; Valenzuela, 1999; Zhou & Bankston, 1998). Some examples include parent and child separation due to immigration and work, language barrier, and parent and child role reversals. As a result, children of immigrants often experience academic, social, and/or emotional difficulties. Research also has shown that students of color perceive a lack of "authentic caring" (Valenzuela, 1999) in the schools, and thus they view schools as a space of "subtractive schooling" (Valenzuela, 1999). I focused on the services and support during out-of-school time (OST) hours that provide them "positive learning opportunities with supportive adults," specifically community-based organizations (CBOs) (Banks et al., 2007, p. 21). This book examines the role and impact of a CBO in family–community–school partnerships and how CBOs provide information, support, and advocacy for low-income Chinese immigrant families.

Since prior research on post-1965 children of immigrants has generally been family and school based, my research looks at the educational, social, and emotional adjustments of these young people by examining their relationship with community-based youth centers. Additionally, much of the previous research on children of immigrants and home–school relations often focuses on describing the barriers faced by parents rather than illustrating specific well-conceived action and strategies. See, for example, the studies cited by Adler (2007), Siu (2002), and Valdés (1996). Most of the home–school relationship strategies use a top-down hierarchical model and cultural deficit framework. Furthermore, CBOs are generally absent and overlooked in the discussion. I argue that the CBO's sensitivity and knowledge of this community and their ability to access the dominant culture were central to their success. I specifically illustrate how the HCCC's CYC assists low-income and working poor children of immigrants and their immigrant parents with information, support, and advocacy.

While it is crucial to provide the codes needed to access and navigate the "culture of power" (Delpit, 1988, 1995), equally important is honoring and upholding the cultural wealth, which I argue HCCC has been doing for more than forty-five years. The role of CBOs in the lives of youth, their families, and schools is significant because these agencies are important factors that work for and with immigrant families and communities. They value the community's rich assets, and are aware of the community's struggles in accessing dominant institutions, such as schools. For instance, HCCC knows how doors operate in dominant institutions and in doing so, HCCC links the community's multiple worlds (Phelan, Davidson, & Yu, 1991, 1993; Phelan et al., 1998) through opening doors, rather than masking, separating, and dehumanizing them. I employed youth (comm)unity (Wong, 2010) and community cultural wealth (Yosso, 2005) as the conceptual frameworks to examine the role and impact of CBOs in family–community–school partnerships.

Youth (comm)unity

Throughout this book, I imagine CYC as a youth (comm)unity space by looking through the lens of three critical concepts. They are (1) the Multiple Worlds model developed by Phelan et al. (1991, 1993, 1998); (2) Angela Valenzuela's authentic caring (1999); and (3) Gloria Ladson-Billings's culturally relevant (1994, 1995a, 1995b) understanding. In doing so, the concept of youth (comm)unity emerges which I argue is key in order to better serve students of color and low-income families. Freire (1996) reminds us that, "Students' learning depends on health and emotional stability" (p. 90), which the youth are able to receive from CYC. Through providing the youth with a sense of youth (comm)unity, CYC is able to offer academic, social, emotional, and leadership developments.

Youth (comm)unity as multiple worlds

The Multiple Worlds model examines the interrelationships between students' family, friends, and school "worlds" through six patterns of transition and adaptation: (1) Congruent Worlds/Smooth Transitions; (2) Different Worlds/ Border Crossings Managed; (3) Different Worlds/Border Crossings Difficult; (4) Different Worlds/Border Crossing Resisted; (5) Congruent Worlds/ Border Crossings Resisted; (6) Different Worlds/Smooth Transitions (Phelan et al., 1998).

The youth in this research closely match the Different Worlds/Border Crossing Managed typology; because even though they view their home and school worlds as distinct from one another, the youth are able to "utilize strategies that enable them to manage crossing successfully" the the assistance of CYC and other CBOs (Phelan et al., 1998, p. 14). CYC, and HCCC as a whole, is a space created by and for the community, and thus able to negotiate and connect the youths' family, friends, and school worlds. In doing so, similar to Bhabha's notion of "third space," CYC represents a new and hybrid space that draws from the youths' multiple worlds. This "third space," Bhabha explains, "enables other positions to emerge" (Rutherford, 1990, p. 211). At the same time, because it is distinct from the space of home and of school where children of immigrants often feel isolated and/or disconnected, CYC builds a sense of community by creating strong (Piha & Adams, 2001), positive, and trusting relationships with youth through a culturally relevant (Ladson-Billings 1994, 1995a, 1995b) understanding.

In a sense, my idea of youth (comm)unity helps low-income Chinese American youth in this research negotiate the "multiple worlds" in what Anzaldúa (1987) refers to as the "borderlands": "a state that exists whenever cultural differences exist, whether those cultures involve physical differences such as race, class or gender or differences that are less tangible-psychological, social, or cultural" (Foss, Foss, & Griffin, 1999, p. 106).

The borderlands have always been present in the United States' long racist history toward communities of color. For example, the Chinese Exclusion Act of 1882 was the first immigration law in U.S. history to target and exclude a specific ethnic group from entering the United States. The Act banned Chinese immigration and essentially forced them into areas that have became known as Chinatown today (see Chapter 2). If we look at today's context, such hatred and racist structures are still prevalent (e.g., English-only movement, the absence of and attacks on Ethnic Studies and anti-racist education in our schools, and the current anti-immigrant movement); and thus affect how schools/dominant culture view our students and their families in classrooms and society. By extending Anzaldúa's concept of "borderlands," I argue that since the young people's home and school worlds are colliding with one another, they are (co)constructing and finding this youth (comm)unity in the "borderlands," where CBOs help the youth negotiate between their family/home culture and school/dominant culture.

Youth (comm)unity as authentic caring

In the case of schools, young people may not feel welcomed if they perceive their teachers and administrators as "uncaring" (Valenzuela, 1999). Valenzuela (1999) found in her research on Mexican American youth in a Houston high school that "schooling is organized in ways that subtract resources from Mexican youth" (p. 10). She argues that students are not opposed to education. Instead they are opposed to the schooling, which is "the content of their education and the way it is offered to them" (Valenzuela, 1999, p. 19). As a result, young people might become resistant and withdraw academically (e.g., cutting classes, not turning in assignments, acting out in classes, dropping out of school, etc.) or in other cases, they simply withdraw socially (Dance, 2002; Lee, 2005; Lew, 2004; Lopez, 2003; Oakes, 1985; Suárez-Orozco & Suárez-Orozco, 2001). For some youth, if they are unable to receive the necessary support then they begin to reject society (Roffman, Suárez-Orozco, & Rhodes, 2003). According to Garrod, Smulyan, Powers, and Kilkenny (1995), "adolescence is a critical stage in the individual's development," where they are "intensely aware of how they are seen by others" (p. 8). Furthermore, if students encounter racism and hostility in the schools, such incidents might fuel them with hopelessness and isolation. It is during such times that they are in search for an alternative supportive structure, such as gang membership (Lay, 2004; Vigil, 1988; Vigil, Yun, & Cheng, 2004), which can provide a sense of support, protection, security, and family.

I, however, will illustrate another sense of family and community formation and authentic caring—that of CBOs. From the interviews and interactions, Valenzuela's concept of "authentic caring" emerged as my collaborators talked about the ways that they felt welcomed, a sense of trust and caring at CYC. In addition, I am extending the concept to include "multi-reciprocal caring relationships." While Valenzuela illustrates authentic caring as reciprocal relationships between school personnel and youth, I will illustrate that authentic caring also occurs between adults and youth *and* youth and youth at CYC. Therefore, "authentic caring" in my research refers to the multi-reciprocal caring relationships in CBOs.

Youth (comm)unity as culturally relevant understanding

Ladson-Billings (1995b) frames culturally relevant pedagogy as "a theoretical model that not only addresses student achievement, but also helps students to accept and affirm their cultural identity while developing critical perspectives that challenge inequalities that schools (and other institutions) perpetuate" (p. 469). While some scholars have argued that culturally sensitive education is important, we need to move toward a culturally relevant education. The main difference between the two is that in a culturally relevant pedagogy, "students must also develop a critical consciousness through which they challenge the status quo of the current social order" (Ladson-Billings, 1995a, p. 160). I argue, therefore, in addition to the two concepts, "culturally relevant" understanding is also a key component in creating a sense of youth (comm)unity.

Community cultural wealth

I employ Yosso's (2005) "community cultural wealth" framework to argue that HCCC helps low-income Chinese immigrant families negotiate and navigate their multiple worlds. Community cultural wealth is defined "as an array of knowledges, skills, abilities, and contacts possessed and used by Communities of Color to survive and resist racism and other forms of oppression" (Yosso & García, 2007, p. 154). The community cultural wealth framework consists of at least six forms of capital that are often overlooked by schools and other institutions: aspirational, navigational, social, linguistic, familial, and resistant capital. "These various forms of capital," as Yosso (2005) stated, "are not mutually exclusive or static, but rather are dynamic processes that build on one another as part of community cultural wealth" (p. 77). Rather than using a top-down hierarchical model and cultural deficit framework (i.e., perceiving difference as a deficit and thus placing the blame on families and communities for inadequacies), HCCC acknowledges the importance of implementing a cultural wealth model in serving the community (Wong, 2008, 2010, 2013). While it is crucial to provide the codes needed to access and navigate U.S. society, equally important is honoring and upholding the families' cultural wealth, which HCCC has been doing for more than forty-five years.

Out-of-school time

The OST hours are "critical hours" (Miller, 2003) for young people, especially since children and youth spend only 20 percent of their time in schools and thus "school time takes up only a fraction of children's [and youths'] social, education, and recreational lives" (Davis & Farbman, 2002, p. 65). Approximately 7 million children in the United States are now regular attendees of an afterschool[1] program between the hours of 3 p.m. and 6 p.m. (Capizzano, Tout, & Adams, 2000). OST settings offer a unique context, and "[b]ecause they are not necessarily associated with the expectations of school or other major institutions, students may feel more at home in intermediary spaces" (Noam, Miller, & Barry, 2002, p. 14). Irby, Pittman, and Tolman (2003) remind us, "schools are only one of a range of learning environments that share responsibility for helping students learn and achieve mastery ... community-based organizations are also themselves settings for learning and engagement" (pp. 18–19). Banks et al. (2007) state "[m]ost of the learning that occurs across the life span takes places in informal environments" (p. 9). Moreover, quality OST programming provides relationships among youth, program staffs, and community leaders (De Jesús, Oviedo, & Feliz, 2015; Woodland, 2008) and various positive educational, emotional, and social developments (Greenberg, 2014; Woodland, 2008; Yu, Newport-Berra, & Liu, 2015).

My research is unique because it broadens the current and narrow home–school relationship paradigm by including the community as another pivotal player in the dialogue and partnership. Prior and current research on OST educational spaces and ASPs are generally in the fields of social work, public health, and psychology, and not education. Additionally, the literature on OSTs is often about improving the academic achievement of "at-risk" students—often Black students—and neglects how their academic experiences intersect with their social and emotional experiences. There is very little comprehensive research that provides detailed portraits of CBOs. This research, therefore, contributes to our understanding of a particular OST program, an ethnic CBO, by examining it through an educational lens and by focusing on youths' academic, social, and emotional experiences. It also emphasizes community-based collaborative approaches, which recognize "community cultural wealth" (Yosso, 2005), "amplify" youth, parental, and family voices (Diniz-Pereira, 2005), and parental agency in serving the community. Another aspect that will set this book apart from others is that it illustrates the intersections of low-income and working-poor immigrant families with U.S. schools, Asian American educational experiences, and the services and support in OST settings, specifically CBOs—an intersection that has not been previously explored.

Post-1965 children of immigrants

The passage of the 1965 Immigration and Naturalization Act (also known as the Hart-Celler Act of 1965) had a significant impact on Asian American immigration to the United States. The Act eliminated the 1924 National Origins Quota System and ended various racist laws that affected the Asian American and Pacific Islander American community, along with other communities of color. Thus, the post-1965 wave of immigration resulted in diversifying the United States.

The two most significant and persistent stereotypes for Asian Americans are the "perpetual foreigner" and the "model minority." The perpetual foreigner or forever foreigners (Suzuki, 1995; Takaki, 2008; Tuan, 1998) stereotype asserts that Asian Americans are un-assimilable foreigners, regardless of how long they have lived in the United States and what generation they are. Thus, the line of "Where are you *really* from?" is a constant racial trauma for Asian Americans, despite their rich history in the United States. Being "foreign" essentially is associated with the "Other" in the dominant racial discourse and as a result, the U.S. American-born students often disassociate themselves from the (recent) immigrant students (or are pressured to do so). That is, in order to conform to or be accepted by the mainstream/ dominant culture, second generation Asian Americans often distanced themselves from the immigrant Asians, who are viewed as the "Other" and "un-American."

Asian Americans are still being portrayed by the dominant culture as a "success story" (i.e., model minority). That is, Asian Americans are stereotyped as the minoritized group that achieves academic success, holds middle-class values of hard work, and are economically successful above all other minoritized groups. This notion ends up harming those Asian Americans who are poor and struggling academically and/or emotionally because the stereotype creates an illusion that Asian American students do not need any type of assistance and support to achieve. Such stereotyping also hides the diversity within the Asian American community. By failing to recognize this diversity, the model minority stereotype allows policy makers as well as service providers to ignore many of their basic needs and often overlook the community as a whole.

The persistent stereotypes of Asian Americans as the model minority (Chang & Au, 2007/2008; Kim & Yeh, 2002; Lee, 1994, 1996; Lee, Wong, & Alvarez, 2008; Wong, 2008) and perpetual foreigner (Tuan, 1998; Wong, 2008; Wu, 2002) add another context/layer to the invisibility. Asian Americans have been broadly portrayed as the U.S.'s "model minority" because of their success, as a group, in attaining high levels of education and career success when compared with members of other racial and ethnic minoritized groups. Thus, the dominant culture have "virtually equated the term, 'Asian American,' with 'success'" (Yun, 1989: p. vii) and offers proof that the U.S. "American Dream" and meritocracy is real and works as intended; and subsequently pits racial and ethnic communities against each another.

Moreover, scholars have mentioned the importance of children of immigrants in community-based youth organizations. In her report on Southeast Asian American students, Yang (2004) notes that "Community-based organizations have been proven to have the ability to provide environments in which Southeast Asian Americans flourish academically, in part by fostering healthy communication between students, parents, and teachers" because these organizations "provide supports that help validate the cultural and historical context of Southeast Asian Americans as they adjust to U.S. society" (p. 129). However, while scholars have noted the importance of CBOs for students of color, there is limited research that looks inside such spaces.

Although the research literature on OST educational spaces is growing, few studies have examined qualitatively *what* these spaces do and *how* they support the youth who participate. Even fewer studies focus on the specific needs of youth from low-income and working-poor immigrant families. Since prior research on children of immigrants has generally been family and school-based, my research looked at the educational, social, and emotional adjustments of these young people by examining their experiences in OST spaces specifically CBOs. Therefore, this book examines the services and support during nonschool hours that assist Asian American youth from low-income and working-poor immigrant families in mediating their multiple worlds.

Methodology and framework

This book is based on an ethnographic research that was conducted in 2004, 2006–2007, and 2015 and consisted of participant observation, document analysis, and open-ended interviews with 38 youth, 14 parents, and 8 HCCC staff members. The staff and youth interviews were conducted in Chinese Cantonese, English, or a mixture of both languages. All of the parent interviews were in Cantonese. I have transcribed the interviews conducted in English verbatim while I have transcribed and translated the interviews conducted in Cantonese, and, thus, these latter transcripts are in the form of "standard English."

I see the youth, parents, and staffs as collaborators rather than participants, informants, or subjects because such a view allows me to, as in Ladson-Billings's work with African-Americans, "work collectively" and "honor ... and benefit" the community (1994, p. 153). I also do not use the term "giving voice" because by using it the assumption is that the "oppressed" (Freire, 1999) do not have a voice and, thus, they must be given permission by an authority (e.g., a researcher) to speak. If researchers are holding to such a belief and mentality then we, too, are guilty of perpetuating oppressive ideology and practices. Rather than "giving voice" to my collaborators, I "amplify" (Diniz-Pereira, 2005) the voices that are too often unheard, marginalized, and ignored by the systems and structures that hold inequality in place. My work amplifies the visibility of Asian Americans, who are not "model minorities," but instead face complex barriers (see Lee et al., 2008; Wong, 2008).

I have made a strong attempt to involve my collaborators as much as possible during this research process. For instance, I provided the staff members a draft of the possible interview questions and asked if there should be any revisions or addendums. In addition, I returned the individual transcripts to the collaborators so they could check for errors in fact, meaning, and expression, especially since I am aware of language differences and the tendency to do drive-by or parachute research in low-income communities and communities of color. In other words, researchers come in as outside experts, collect data, leave, and/or do not give back to the individuals and/or community.

The CYC staff members

I interviewed eight current and two former HCCC staff members in 2004 and 2006–2007. The staff members' diverse racial, ethnic, and national backgrounds and immigration experiences shape the work at CYC and HCCC. Some of the staffs were former participants of HCCC and CYC while others volunteered or were new. Nonetheless, all of them bring a unique experience and their commitment and passion for youth and community work were visible.

All of the staffs were first, 1.5, or second generation children of immigrants of color. They were all college graduates and many were the first in their family to attend and graduate from college. The majority of the staffs have been a part of HCCC for at least five years, with a number having been there for more than ten years. Moreover, a number of the staffs majored, minored, or took classes in Asian American Studies, which illustrates the significance of and need for Ethnic Studies. While they each might have had their own reasons for doing community work and working with youth from immigrant families, the staff members all love teaching and learning from young people. For instance, they shared similar childhood experiences with the youth, wanted to serve the community, or recognized the importance of creating a space for young people to empower themselves.

The youth and parents

At the time of this research all of the youth, ages 12–20, attend(ed) urban public schools in or right outside Harborview. They either attended traditional public secondary schools or elite public high schools that required a competitive exam and high GPA for admission. The size of the schools varied (e.g., from 50 to over 300 students per grade level). All of the youth at CYC came from homes in which Cantonese, Fujianese, Mandarin, and/or Toisanese are the language used for communication. Out of the 14 parents, there were 12 mothers and 2 fathers. Interviews with parents were conducted in 2006–2007. As Table 1.1 indicates, the parents were all first generation immigrants from Guangdong and Fukien Provinces of Mainland China or Hong Kong.

Table 1.1: Parents.

Name	Age	Place of Birth	Children (Age)	Current Occupation	Highest Education Level	Years in United States
Mrs. Liao	43	Guangdong Province, China	Bebe* (18) Yee-Mun* (18)	Assembly worker, Food packaging factory	High school	1
Mrs. Zhang	41	Guangdong Province, China	Jason* (16)	Supermarket Chain	Some high school	1
Mr. Zhang	45			Elder care assistant	Some high school	1
Mrs. Mui	44	Guangdong Province, China	Betty* (12)	Hotel housekeeper	High school	7
Mr. Mui	47			Stocker, Co-ethnic market	High school	2
Mrs. Lau	39	Guangdong Province, China	Samantha* (13) David (9)	Hotel housekeeper	Some high school	4
Mrs. Ho	40	Guangdong Province, China	Jerry* (12) Susan (7)	Co-ethnic restaurant	Some junior high	4
Mrs. Wu	34	Fukien Province, China	Calvin* (12)	Co-ethnic restaurant	Junior high school	4
Mrs. Cheung	50	Hong Kong	David* (19) Steven* (17)	Assembly worker, Electronic factory	Junior high school	5
Mrs. Wong	45	Guangdong Province, China	Joe* (18)	Hotel housekeeper	High school	5 ½
Mrs. Yee	41	Guangdong Province, China	Peter* (14) David (12)	Medical assistant, Community clinic	Some college	15

Table 1.1: (*Continued*).

Name	Age	Place of Birth	Children (Age)	Current Occupation	Highest Education Level	Years in United States
Ms. Chan	41	Vietnam—grew up in Guangdong Province, China	Samuel* (14) Philip* (18)	Data entry, private company	Some high school	18
Mrs. Kam	49	Guangdong Province, China	Ben (18) Vincent* (16)	Data entry, private company	High school	18
Mrs. Lee	51	Guangdong Province, China	Albert* (20) Marc* (17)	Assembly Worker, Food Packaging Factory	High school	21

*Youth who have/had participated in YC events.

The activist scholar

As an activist scholar of color, my degrees "never belonged solely to us or was just for our individual benefit"; rather "we viewed our degrees as belonging to our communities and as being connected to the collective and historical struggle to eliminate the injustices in schools and the larger society" (Wong, 2017, p. 85). We hold ourselves responsible for bridging research, teaching, and activism. As Ladson-Billings (2000) eloquently reminds us, "My research is a part of my life and my life is a part of my research" (p. 268). Having been involved in community and youth work for close to twenty years, I am committed to constructing collaborative research that works for and with communities of color, addressing their experiences with the goal of justice that improves the lives of the community. Having grown up in Harborview, I was able to negotiate entry in certain aspects that might be difficult for someone who was not from the community. For example, I was introduced to Wai-Ming, who was the Director of CYC at the time, through a childhood friend, who was a part of CYC and later worked as a youth staff during the summers. Thus, through my childhood friend, I was able to communicate with Wai-Ming and the other staff more easily. Throughout this book, specifically in Chapter 2, I will also add my personal narratives and memories as a reflective process (in italics), because this community is a part of me.

Organization of the book

Chapter 1 introduces the reader to conversations about OST educational spaces and CBOs, explains how this research fits within and adds to the literature on family and community studies, youth development, and the education of children of immigrants, specifically Asian American youth, as it connects with out-of-school learning, and how HCCC fits into that context. I imagine HCCC as a youth (comm)unity space by utilizing Yosso's (2005) community cultural wealth and examining through the lens of three critical concepts: (1) the Multiple Worlds model developed by Phelan et al. (1991, 1993, 1998); (2) Angela Valenzuela's authentic caring (1999); and (3) Gloria Ladson-Billings's culturally relevant (1994, 1995a, 1995b) understanding. In doing so, the concept of "youth (comm)unity" emerges, which I argue is key in order to better serve low-income students of color. It also provides an overview of the rest of the book. Chapter 2 sketches the portraits of the various settings that make up this research: begins with illustrating the different images of Chinatown and then moving to the richness as well as the struggles of Harborview's Chinatown, HCCC, and CYC.

Chapters 3 and 4 highlight the experiences of first, 1.5, and second generation Chinese American young people and their immigrant parents in the United States and U.S. schools. Chapter 3 provides a glimpse of the triangulated dilemmas between low-income immigrant parents' levels of knowledge about U.S. schools that are often taken for granted by those who know *and* have access to the system. As a result, parents felt disconnected from their children's school. Schools are inaccessible institutional sites for parents. This chapter illustrates the parents' relationship with their children and U.S. schools. Chapter 4 examines the youths' relationship with their immigrant parents and U.S. schools. In doing so, these chapters as well as the entire book amplifies (Diniz-Pereira, 2005, 2006) the voices of Asian American young people and their immigrant families.

Chapters 5 and 6 illustrate the services and support that HCCC's youth program, CYC, offers to the youth, their families, and the Asian American community in the Harborview area. Chapter 5 shows how CYC serves as a triangulated bridge as the young people and their immigrant parents try to understand the dominant U.S. culture and, at the same time, they try to understand each other and themselves. In other words, it explores the role and impact of an urban CBO and its youth program in assisting and providing information, support, and advocacy for low-income and working poor Chinese immigrant families. In essence, CYC plays a dual role in helping low-income and working-class Chinese American young people *and* their immigrant parents bridge the intergenerational gap between the two. CYC also helps the youth and their families negotiate a system that is not necessarily familiar and transparent for them. In doing so, CYC links the three worlds or "multiple worlds." I suggest CYC offers the young people and their families the codes, or rules, needed to access and navigate the "culture of power" (Delpit, 1988, 1995), while also honoring and upholding their community capital. Chapter 6 describes how CYC bridges the youths' "multiple worlds," by providing a space I call "youth (comm)unity" for youth from low-income Chinese immigrant families in the Harborview area.

Chapter 7 revisits some of the young people who participated in CYC nine years ago and are now "CYC alums." All of the young people have graduated from high school and are pursuing higher education, hold a bachelor's degree, and/or work full-time. Finally, Chapter 8 summarizes the entire book and outlines the educational policy implementations and possible future research based on the findings of this research.

Note

1. According to Noam et al. (2002), the difference between the terms after-school and after-school is the following: the term afterschool (i.e., one word) "conveys the institutional legitimacy of the field rather than a tangential add-on to the institution of school" (p. 18). Throughout this book, I will use the terms "afterschools" and "after-schools" interchangeably in referring to the programs and services that are held after school. When quoting others, I will maintain its original usage.

Works cited

Adler, S. M. (2007). Hmong home-school relations: Hmong parents and professionals speak out. In C. C. Park, R. Endo, S. J. Lee, & X. L. Rong (Eds.), *Asian American education: Acculturation, literacy development, and learning* (pp. 77–104). Charlotte, NC: Information Age Publishing.

Anzaldúa, G. (1987). *Borderlands/la frontera: The new mestiza*. San Francisco, CA: Aunt Lute.

Banks, J. A., Au, K. A., Ball, A. F., Bell, P., Gordon, E. W., Gutierrez, K. D., ... Zhou, M. (2007). *Learning in and out of school in diverse environments: Life-long, life-wide, life-deep*. Seattle, WA: Center for Multicultural Education and The LIFE Center.

Bhabha, H. K. (1990). Interview with Homi Bhabha: The third space. In J. Rutherford (Ed.), *Identity: Community, culture and difference* (pp. 207–221). London: Lawrence and Wishart.

Capizzano, J., Tout, K., & Adams, G. (2000). *Child care patterns of school-age children with employed mothers*. Washington, DC: Urban Institute.

Chang, B., & Au, W. (2007/2008, Winter). You're Asian, How could you fail math? Unmasking the myth of the model minority. *Rethinking Schools, 22*(2), 15–18.

Dance, L. J. (2002). *Tough fronts: The impact of street culture on schooling*. New York, NY: RoutledgeFalmer.

Davis, J., & Farbman, D. A. (2002, Summer). Schools alone are not enough: After-school programs and education reform in Boston. *Youth Development and After-School Time: A Tale of Many Cities* (pp. 65–88). New Directions for Youth Development: Theory Practice Research, No. 94. San Francisco, CA: Jossey-Bass.

De Jesús, A., Oviedo, S., & Feliz, S. (2015). Global kids organizing in the global city: Generation of social capital in a youth organizing program. *Afterschool Matters, 21*, 20–28.

Delpit, L. (1988). The silenced dialogue: Power and pedagogy in educating other people's children. *Harvard Educational Review, 58*(3), 280–298.

Delpit, L. (1995). *Other people's children: Cultural conflict in the classroom*. New York, NY: The New Press.

Diniz-Pereira, J. E. (2005). *"How the dreamers are born"—The identity construction of activist educators: Life histories of women educators from the Landless Workers Movement in Brazil* (Doctoral dissertation). Department of Curriculum and Instruction, University of Wisconsin-Madison.

Diniz-Pereira, J. E. (2006, April 7–11). *Critical life history inquiry and the identity construction of activist educators in Brazil.* Paper presented at the 2006 American Educational Research Association Annual Meeting, San Francisco, CA.

Foss, K. A., Foss, S. K., & Griffin, C. L. (1999). *Feminist rhetorical theories.* Thousand Oaks, CA: Sage Publications.

Freire, P. (1996). *Letters to Cristina: Reflections of my life and work*. New York, NY: Routledge.

Freire, P. (1999). *Pedagogy of the oppressed*. New York, NY: The Continuum Publishing.

Garrod, A., Smulyan, L., Powers, S. I., & Kilkenny, R. (1995). *Adolescent portraits: Identity, relationships, and challenges* (2nd ed.). Needham Heights, MA: Allyn & Bacon.

Gibson, M. A. (1988). *Accommodation without assimilation: Sikh immigrants in an American high school*. Ithaca, NY: Cornell University Press.

Greenberg, J. P. (2014). Significance of after-school programming for immigrant children during middle childhood: Opportunities for school social work. *Social Work, 59*(3), 243–251.

Irby, M., Pittman, K. J., & Tolman, J. (2003, Spring). Blurring the lines: Expanding learning opportunities for children and youth. In M. Irby, K. J. Pittman, & J. Tolman (Eds.), *When, where, what and how youth learn: Blurring school and community boundaries* (pp. 13–28). New Directions for Youth Development: Theory Practice Research, No. 97. San Francisco, CA: Jossey-Bass.

Kim, A., & Yeh, C. (2002). Stereotypes of Asian American Students. *Eric Digest*, No. 172.

Ladson-Billings, G. (1994). *Dreamkeepers: Successful teachers of African American children*. San Francisco, CA: Jossey-Bass.

Ladson-Billings, G. (1995a). But that's just good teaching! The case for culturally relevant pedagogy. *Theory Into Practice, 34*(3), 159–165.

Ladson-Billings, G. (1995b, Fall). Toward a theory of culturally relevant pedagogy. *American Educational Research Journal, 32*(3), 465–491.

Ladson-Billings, G. (2000). Racialized discourses and ethnic epistemologies. In N. K. Denzin & Y. S. Lincoln (Eds.), *Handbook of qualitative research* (2nd ed., pp. 257–277). Thousand Oaks, CA: Sage Publications.

Lay, S. (2004). Lost in the fray: Cambodian American youth in providence, Rhode Island. In J. Lee & M. Zhou (Eds.), *Asian American youth: Culture, identity, and ethnicity* (pp. 221–231). New York, NY: Routledge.

Lee, S. J. (1994). Behind the model-minority stereotype: Voices of high- and low-achieving Asian American students. *Anthropology & Education Quarterly, 25*(4), 413–429.

Lee, S. J. (1996). *Unraveling the model minority stereotype: Listening to Asian American youth.* New York, NY: Teachers College Press.

Lee, S. J. (2001). More than "model minorities" or "delinquents": A look at Hmong American high school students. *Harvard Educational Review, 71*(3), 505–528.

Lee, S. J. (2005). *Up against Whiteness: Race, school and immigrant youth.* New York, NY: Teachers College Press.

Lee, S. J., Wong, N. W. A., & Alvarez, A. N. (2008). The model minority and the perpetual foreigner: Stereotypes of Asian Americans. In N. Tewari & A. N. Alvarez (Eds.), *Asian American psychology: Current perspectives* (pp. 69–84). New York, NY: Lawrence Erlbaum.

Lew, J. (2003). The (re)construction of second-generation ethnic networks: Structuring academic success of Korean American high school students. In C. C. Park, A. L. Goodwin, & S. J. Lee (Eds.), *Asian American identities, families, and schooling* (pp. 157–176). Greenwich, CT: Information Age Publishing.

Lew, J. (2004). The "other" story of model minorities: Korean American high school dropouts in an urban context. *Anthropology & Education Quarterly, 35*(3), 303–323.

Lew, J. (2006). *Asian Americans in class: Charting the achievement gap among Korean American youth.* New York, NY: Teachers College Press.

Li, G. (2003). Literacy, culture, and politics of schooling: Counternarratives of a Chinese Canadian Family. *Anthropology & Education Quarterly, 34*(2), 184–206.

Lopez, N. (2003). *Hopeful girls, troubled boys: Race and gender disparity in urban education.* New York, NY: Routledge.

Louie, V. S. (2004). *Compelled to excel: Immigration, education, and opportunity among Chinese Americans.* Stanford, CA: Stanford University Press.

Miller, B. (2003). *Critical hours: Afterschool programs and educational success.* Quincy, MA: Nellie Mae Education Foundation.

Noam, G. G., Miller, B. M., & Barry, S. (2002, Summer). Youth development and after-school time: A tale of many cities. In G. G. Noam & B. M. Miller (Eds.), *Youth development and afterschool time: Policy and programming in large cities* (pp. 9–18). New Directions for Youth Development: Theory Practice Research, No. 94. San Francisco, CA: Jossey-Bass.

Oakes, J. (1985). *Keeping track: How schools structure inequality.* New Haven, CT: Yale University Press.

Olsen, L. (1997). *Made in America: Immigrant students in our public schools.* New York, NY: New Press.

Pang, V. O., Kiang, P. N., & Pak, Y. K. (2004). Asian Pacific American students: Challenging a biased educational system. In J. A. Banks & C. A. McGee Banks (Eds.), *Handbook of research on multicultural education* (2nd ed., pp. 542–563). San Francisco, CA: Jossey-Bass.

Phelan, P., Davidson, A. L., & Yu, H. C. (1991). Students' multiple worlds: Negotiating the boundaries of family, peer, and school cultures. *Anthropology & Education Quarterly, 22*(3), 224–250.

Phelan, P., Davidson, A. L., & Yu, H. C. (1993). Students' multiple worlds: Navigating the borders of family, peer, and the school cultures. In P. Phelan & A. L. Davidson (Eds.), *Renegotiating cultural diversity in American school* (pp. 52–88). New York, NY: Teachers College Press.

Phelan, P., Davidson, A. L., & Yu, H. C. (1998). *Adolescents' worlds: Negotiating family, peers, and school.* New York, NY: Teachers College Press.

Piha, S., & Adams, A. (2001). *Youth development guide: Engaging young people in after-school programming.* San Francisco, CA: Community Network for Youth Development.

Roffman, J. G., Suárez-Orozco, C., & Rhodes, J. E. (2003). Facilitating positive development in immigrant youth: The role of mentors and community organizations. In F. A. Villarruel, D. F. Perkins, L. M. Borden, & J. G. Keith (Eds.), *Community youth development: Programs, policies, and practices* (pp. 90–117). Thousand Oaks, CA: Sage Publications.

Siu, S. F. (2002). Toward building home-school partnerships: The case of Chinese American families and public schools. In E. H. Tamura, V. Chattergy, & R. Endo (Eds.), *Asian and Pacific Islander American education: Social, cultural, and historical contexts* (pp. 59–84). South El Monte, CA: Pacific Asia Press.

Stanton-Salazar, R. D. (2001). *Manufacturing hope and despair: The school and kin support networks of U.S.-Mexican youth.* New York, NY: Teachers College Press.

Suárez-Orozco, C., & Suárez-Orozco, M. M. (2001). *Children of immigration.* Cambridge, MA: Harvard University Press.

Suzuki, B. (1995). Education and the socialization of Asian Americans: A revisionist analysis of the "Model Minority" thesis. In D. T. Nakanishi & T. Y. Nishida (Eds.), *The Asian American educational experience: A sourcebook for teachers and students* (pp. 113–132). New York, NY: Routledge.

Takaki, R. (2008). *A different mirror: A history of multicultural America.* New York, NY: Back Bay Books/Little, Brown, and Co.

Tuan, M. (1998). *Forever foreigners or honorary Whites? The Asian ethnic experience today.* New Brunswick, NJ: Rutgers University Press.

Valdés, G. (1996). *Con respecto: Bridging the distances between culturally diverse families and schools.* New York, NY: Teachers College Press.

Valdés, G. (2001). *Learning and not learning English: Latino students in American schools.* New York, NY: Teachers College Press.

Valenzuela, A. (1999). *Subtractive schooling: U.S.-Mexican youth and the politics of caring.* Albany, NY: State of New York Press.

Vigil, J. D. (1988). *Barrio gangs: Street life and identity in Southern California.* Austin, TX: University of Texas Press.

Vigil, J. D., Yun, S. C., & Cheng, J. (2004). A shortcut to the American dream? Vietnamese youth gangs in Little Saigon. In J. Lee & M. Zhou (Eds.), *Asian American youth: Culture, identity, and ethnicity* (pp. 207–219). New York, NY: Routledge.

Wong, N. W. A. (2008). "They see us as resource": The role of a community-based youth center in supporting the academic lives of low-income Chinese American Youth. *Anthropology & Education Quarterly, 39*(2), 181–204.

Wong, N. W. A. (2010). "Cuz they care about the people who goes there": The multiple roles of a community-based youth center in providing "Youth (Comm)Unity" for low-income Chinese American youth. *Urban Education, 45*(5), 708–739.

Wong, N. W. A. (2013). "Like a bridge": How a community-based organization helps immigrant and working poor Chinese parents navigate U.S. schools. In R. Endo & X. L. Rong (Eds.), *Educating Asian Americans: Achievement, schooling, and identities* (pp. 181–204). Charlotte, NC: Information Age Publishing.

Wong, N. W. A. (2017). "Lovely to me": An immigrant's daughter's critical self-reflexivity research journey. *Journal of Critical Thought and Praxis, 6*(2), 84–94.

Woodland, D. H. (2008). Whatcha doin' after school? A review of the literature on the influence of after-school programs on young Black males. *Urban Education, 43*(5), 537–560.

Wu, F. H. (2002). *Yellow: Race in America beyond Black and White*. New York, NY: Basic Books.

Yang, K. Y. (2004). Southeast Asian American children: Not the "model minority". *The Future of Children: Children of Immigrant Families, 14*(2), 127–133.

Yosso, T. (2005). Whose culture has capital? A critical race theory discussion of community cultural wealth. *Race, Ethnicity and Education, 8*(1), 69–91.

Yosso, T., & García, D. (2007). "This is no slum!" A critical race theory analysis of community cultural wealth in culture clash's Chavez Ravine. *Aztlan: A Journal of Chicano Studies, 32*(1), 145–179.

Yu, S. M., Newport-Berra, M., & Liu, J. (2015). Out-of-school time activity participation among U.S.-immigrant youth. *Journal of School Health, 85*(5), 281–288.

Yun, G. (1989). Introduction. In G. Yun (Ed.), *A look beyond the model minority image: Critical issues in Asian America*. Hamden, CT: Minority Rights Group.

Zhou, M., & Bankston III, C. L. (1998). *Growing up American: How Vietnamese adopt to life in the United States*. New York, NY: Russell Stage Foundation.

CHAPTER TWO

Portraits of Chinatown, Harborview, and HCCC

My family has a long history in the U.S. However, due to federal policies like the 1882 Chinese Exclusion Act that singled out Chinese on the basis of ethnicity, my ancestors were denied the right to citizenship and the opportunity to bring families to the U.S. In 1882, the Chinese Exclusion Act became the first federal policy to single out a specific group of people from entering the U.S., simply because of their ethnicity, race, or religion. While my parents came to the U.S. after 1965, my family's history in the U.S. and Canada dates back to the late 1800s and early 1900s when my paternal great great-grandfathers came to the U.S. and Canada and worked in the laundry and restaurant industries. My ngeen ngeen's (paternal grandmother in Toisanese) grandfather and three granduncles came to the United States as paper sons in the late 1800s. They settled in Harborview's Chinatown and, like many Chinese men, entered the service sector, working as cooks and launderers due to housing and labor discrimination. According to my ngeen ngeen, due to the hostilities towards Chinese, great great-grandfather felt life in the U.S. would be too harsh for his family and thus, similar to many Chinese men during this time, he left his family in China and sent money back to them whenever possible. Then, as a result of the Chinese Exclusion Act of 1882, my ngeen ngeen's grandfather never returned home to China once he left. Today, let us realize such policy and the racist rhetoric in establishing and justifying fear and hysteria against an entire group of people. The current Muslim ban by the current administration is a stark reminder of the U.S.'s past with excluding Chinese.

Competing images of Chinatown

Chinatowns generally are viewed through two lenses: the dominant lens and the community lens. I argue while the former is pervasive the latter is reality. Chinatowns have always been known as places of exotic customs, sights, and smells. As other scholars have written, Chinatowns and the experiences of Chinese Americans remain hidden or are misinterpreted (Kwong, 1979; Loo, 1991). The stereotypical images of dark and mysterious alleyways filled the dominant culture's historic perceptions of Chinatowns nationwide. The images of "Orientals," "Barbarians," "Coolies," or "Chinamen" with their buckteeth, slanted almond-shaped eyes and strange queues gambling in secret underworlds or lying helplessly in opium-smoked dens are just some of the caricature representations. While the poisons have taken and mesmerized the men's souls, prostitutes lined the doorways trying to lure men, and the aroma of chop suey filled the air. Or they were viewed as cheap labor who "remained the least respected of men" and "remained virtually faceless" (Chu, 1974, p. 63). Dominant U.S. Americans perceived Chinatowns as "depraved colonies of prostitutes, gamblers and opium addicts bereft of decency" (Wu, 2014). In contrast to the stereotypical portraits and misconceptions, Chinatown is a physical, social, emotional, and educational space (Kwong, 1979, 1987; Loo, 1991; Sung, 1972, 1987; To & CHS New England, 2008; Yung & CHSA, 2006; Zhou, 1992). For instance, rather than the "static and antiquated" and "docile, apolitical, and uncommunicative" misconceptions of Chinatowns given by dominant society, Kwong (1979) included a "new and more dynamic perspective" of New York's Chinatown by reconstructing the history (pp. 148, 149, respectively).

As a result of xenophobia toward Chinese and other Asian groups, a series of harsh laws and court decisions were passed in the United States that drastically restricted immigration from Asia. For example, the Chinese Exclusion Act of 1882 prohibited the immigration of Chinese laborers[1] as well as the Chinese from becoming naturalized U.S. citizens, a ban that lasted over sixty years. The act also was the first immigration law in U.S. history to target a specific ethnic group from immigrating to the United States. Due to exclusion, racism, and discrimination during this period, Asians and Asian Americans, the majority being men, were forced to live in segregated, dehumanized, and emasculated worlds. Therefore, while women contributed to community formation (Glenn, 1985), Chinatowns were known as a "Bachelor Society" because Asian women were prohibited from entering the country, and thus directly condemned Asian men's ability to marry and establish family. Moreover, due to anti-miscegenation laws, Asian men were prohibited from marrying U.S. American (White) women in many states. Even further, the Cable Act of 1922 specified that any U.S. American woman who married "an alien ineligible to citizenship" would have their U.S. citizenship revoked, which included Asians (Takaki, 1998, p. 15). Reports of anti-Asian hostility and oppression and physical violence were common, such as burnings of businesses and beatings of Chinese occurred daily if they stepped beyond the Chinatown boundaries (Loo, 1991; Wong, 2006; Yuan, 1963). At the same time, as a result of the discriminatory acts, ethnic enclaves served as a resource and refuge for the "Other" to live, work, seek protection, and survive because for "almost a century, whites refused to work alongside the Chinese" (Kwong, 1997, p. 113). In order to serve the population, Chinatown residents and community members established social and political networks and institutions (e.g., the Chinese Consolidated Benevolent Association) within the community, which are still visible today.

More importantly, the passage of the 1965 Immigration and Naturalization Act (also known as the Hart-Celler Act of 1965) had a significant impact on Chinese American immigration to the United States. The 1965 Immigration and Naturalization Act eliminated the 1924 National Origins Quota System and ended various racist laws that affected the Asian American and Pacific Islander community, along with other communities of color. More than half of the youths' families in this research are from southern China and all came to the United States as a result of the 1965 Act's family reunification preference.

> In the 1970s and 1980s, my family came through the family reunification preference under the 1965 Immigration and Naturalization Act when my paternal aunt sponsored her entire family, which included her parents (my paternal grandparents: yeh yeh, paternal grandfather in Cantonese, and ngeen ngeen) and her six younger siblings. My family eventually settled down in Harborview. My father's side of the family all lived in the same apartment complex while I was growing up. On the weekends, after a long week of work and/or school, the entire family would all have dinner at my grandparents' and then watch Chinese movies and play mahjong.

*****

Today, the images of roast ducks, pigs, and octopus hanging in store windows, tanks filled with live seafood in markets, or dim sum dishes fill the dominant culture's image of Chinatowns. However, as scholars have noted, Chinatowns were and still are places that provide homes, jobs, loans, learning, social and cultural events, safety, and trust.

A portrait of Harborview's Chinatown

Harborview's Chinatown, similar to other parts of the city, is situated on landfill built on tidal flats in the early 1800s in order to provide additional housing for the city's expanding middle-class population. During the 1860s, due to the rise of nativism in the West Coast and following the completion of the transcontinental railroad, Chinese immigrants, most of them from China's Guangdong province, fled and arrived in the East Coast in greater numbers. Increased hostility toward the Chinese was also visible in many of the cities and towns. The area that is now Chinatown has always been a working-class immigrant community surrounded by factories and its proximity to transportation. Today, a number of the buildings, which date back to the early to mid-1800s, are still occupied. At the same time, urban renewal and gentrification has significantly impacted the community. Chinatown has been continuously taken advantage of by both public government agencies and private corporations. Chinatown remains ignored and silenced.

Urban renewal and gentrification

Prior to World War II, Chinatown was relatively small in size and population due to the harsh laws against the Chinese. However, Chinatown was a growing community especially after World War II when family reunifications and the growth in Chinese businesses, particularly restaurants, flourished. Similar to other parts of the country, Chinese American veterans in Harborview were now able to bring their families over, which led to a major population boom in the area during the 1960s.

Since the 1950s, the Chinatown community became a victim of urban renewal, gentrification, and continued institutional racism. Harborview's Chinatown has always been prime property for housing and businesses. U.S. cities such as Harborview adopted strategies to attract businesses and industries back into downtown, to restore its tax base and to attract its residents to stay. As a result, Chinatown has lost one-half of its original land and one-third of its housing to urban renewal and gentrification. "Gentrification," Older (2014) explains, "is violence. Couched in white supremacy, it is a systemic, intentional process of uprooting communities." Furthermore, Park and Leonard state in detail (as quoted by Older, 2014):

> Gentrification represents a socio-historic process where rising housing costs, public policy, persistent segregation, and racial animus facilitates the influx of wealthier, mostly white, residents into a particular neighborhood. Celebrated as 'renewal' and an effort to 'beautify' these communities, gentrification results in the displacement of residents. This has disproportionately impacted communities of color.

Residents living in Harborview's Chinatown, similar to many low-income and working-class communities of color across the United States, are being dispersed, pushed out, and displaced due to gentrification. Additionally, Chinatown is the only neighborhood at the juncture of two major interstate highways intersecting Harborview. In the 1950s construction of the two highways began. One of the highways was not intended to pass through Chinatown, rather it was supposed to run slightly east of Chinatown. However, as a result of heavy protest from local businesses in the 1950s, the city immediately changed its plan and rerouted the highway through Chinatown. Again, Chinatown was ignored and silenced.

Chinatown was affected when the city took land away and sold it to a world-class hospital and a private university during the 1960s and 1970s. Later, the two institutions became partners where the hospital is the principal teaching hospital for the university's medical schools. Even though the medical institution is located in Chinatown, many in the community argue it has not been a part of the community. One community member asserted, "They were in the community. They weren't a part of the community. You know there's a distinct difference with that. And that's how [the medical institution] always was." Thus, while a world-class medical institution sits in Chinatown, it is not there to serve the members of the community. Prior to the construction of these two large institutions, a long negotiation process occurred with community members into the 1990s. According to the agreement, the institutions would provide funds for constructing a new community center and affordable housing in Chinatown. However, the promise did not become reality until almost forty years later with the opening of a recreational facility in 2000.

The expansions of these institutions from the 1960s to the present day, as a result, have enabled the medical institution and university to triple in size. This process, along with the two interstate highways, took over half of Chinatown's land and has isolated the residents into halves, creating a northern (known mostly as the center of Chinatown) and a southern section. Additionally, the interstate highways and medical institutions are also responsible for the serious air pollution, intense traffic congestions, and lack of open space in Chinatown. Harborview Chinatown has only 2.9 acres of open space, which is a mere 0.6 acre per 1,000 residents. Chinatown has the least amount of open space per resident in the city. Once again, Chinatown was ignored and silenced.

Then in the 1970s, the city moved the adult entertainment district (i.e., red light district) to Chinatown in order to make way for the construction of the city's new civic center. The red light district—with its peep shows, pornographic bookstores, striptease clubs, and X-rated movie theaters as well as prostitutes and criminals—consisted of several side streets and one main street. The Hope Elementary School, a public elementary school where many of the Community Youth Center (CYC) youth also attended, was located on the main street and just a few blocks away.

*****

I attended Pre-Kindergarten (Pre-K) and part of 1st grade through 5th grade at the Hope Elementary School during the mid-80s to early-90s. From Pre-K to 2nd grade, my yeh yeh or goo jeh (father's younger sister in Cantonese) would walk my gor gor (older brother) and me to and from school. It was about a 10-minute walk. Getting to and from there, we had to cross 5 major streets with busy intersections. Each day, we would pass by a small playground. Along the way, I would see six to ten used condoms on the sidewalks. Some were found near the swing sets. We would also walk pass prostitutes, who stood across the street from our elementary school in their colorful and glittery mini dresses and high heels. I remember seeing them even in the winter months when the temperatures were in the single digits. It was not until the second grade that I realized what was actually happening.

Hope Elementary School

Serving the Chinatown community and two neighboring communities is Hope Elementary School. Opened in 1976 as a community school, Hope Elementary School is a public Pre-Kindergarten (Pre-K) to fifth grade school with a bright multileveled building. The two interstate highways are within walking distance to the school. The school is an open-space school, where almost all of the classrooms do not have doors. Instead, classrooms are separated with furniture such as low bookshelves. Due to the lack of space in Chinatown, the three level play areas are located on the school's rooftop. During recess, students would be running around or playing in the playground, which was built in 1998. At other times, Harborview Chinatown Community Center (HCCC) and other nonprofits use it either for events (e.g., street fairs) or sport activities (e.g., soccer, badminton, and volleyball). On the lower level are the gym, one full size swimming pool, and a mini pool, which the school shares with HCCC and the general public. The city has designated Hope Elementary School as a training site for teachers and administrators. With the passage of the State's referendum to eliminate bilingual education almost two decades ago, Hope Elementary School is designated as a "language center" where K-5 grade students interested in continuing bilingual education in Chinese may transfer to this school so long as they apply and are approved for waivers. Opened in 1999 as a pilot school, Hope Secondary School emerged from parents and family members' desire for a grade 6–12 school that would continue the educational and cultural atmosphere their children had experienced at Hope Elementary School. In 2006, the school held its first-ever graduating senior class with over thirty students.

*****

My parents enrolled my gor gor and me in the bilingual education program at the Hope Elementary School. I was in the bilingual program from pre-K and then part of first grade to fourth grade. In fifth grade, I went to the English-speaking classroom. I remember learning how to tie my shoelace in pre-K. That night I was so excited that I tied all of the shoes in our apartment while my mommie sat on the living room floor next to me with all the tied shoes lined up.

Since gor gor and I were in the bilingual program, all of our classroom teachers and aides were 1st, 1.5, or 2nd generation Chinese American except for our elective teachers (e.g., art, computer lab, gym, and music), who were all White. At that time, the principal was Mr. Wong, a Chinese American in his 30s, who had been the principal for quite some time and was a well-known person in the community. Mr. Wong always greeted us whenever he passed by our classrooms or if he saw us in the hallways or out at recess. All of our classroom teachers were Cantonese speakers along with the aides, who were usually in their late forties to seventies. The aides taught us Chinese and also assisted the classroom teacher. I remember my classmates and I were pretty close to many of our classroom teachers and aides and I felt that they cared about us. For instance, I remember that my first grade teacher Ms. Shee would spend an hour almost everyday after school with me working on vowels and pronunciations because there was no speech language pathologist and specialist at the school. Or when Yeung bak bak (male elder in Cantonese Chinese), our fourth grade aide, would converse with us about life and would frequently sneak the Marukawa fruit flavor round bubble gum packaged in small square boxes into our pockets as Mr. Chan, our classroom teacher, was writing on the blackboard.

Every year the entire school would celebrate cultural events such as the Lunar New Year. Students, their families, and people from the community would be invited to watch students perform the various Chinese dances and instruments in the gym. These were my happiest years. I remember playing tag, Chinese jump rope, hopscotch, kickball, and basketball during recess. We also played jacks, the various board and card games (e.g., Monopoly, Uno, Othello, and Connect Four).

Having teachers who spoke Cantonese and understood our home culture and family background—the majority of the students were from low-income and working-class immigrant and refugee families—helped my parents understand the U.S. educational system better. All of our report cards, memos, and announcements from the school were in Chinese and English. We also saw our teachers quite often outside the school setting and in the community, such as going to dim sum or dinner or at the local Chinese grocery markets and pastry shops. Even today, I would see many of my teachers when I am in Harborview. My schooling experience at Hope Elementary was in sync with my family culture. During my elementary school years, I was never ashamed of my identity. I was proud of my Chinese American culture, my Chinese name, and being Chinese and Asian American.

*****

The school site also houses two nonprofit agencies on the ground level, a multilingual community health center and HCCC. The community health center, which began in the early 1970s, is the largest Asian community health center in the state.

When I was attending Hope Elementary School, the school nurse's office was one of the offices inside the clinic. I remember entering the clinic through one of the school doors. As a five year old, going to the school nurse's office was like going through a secret passageway because the school magically transformed into the health clinic simply by opening a colorful door. Besides not feeling well, we would see the school nurse for our annual eye and ear check-ups. Today, my ngeen ngeen still goes to the clinic.

According to Susan, HCCC's Executive Director at the time of the research, the community needed the health clinic because "there wasn't language appropriate health services available" at the time. For instance, there were not many translators at the medical institution that spoke Cantonese, Mandarin, and Vietnamese. However, for the past 10 to 15 years, Susan noted that the medical institution has been changing their presence in the community: "they are trying to create jobs, they start investing in the community, they give grants to community-based organizations, [and] they are looking at health disparity issues in the population."

While the medical institution has been making an effort to change their presence in the community, Chinatown residents often prefer the multilingual and multicultural services that the community health clinic offers. For instance, in early April 2008, one of my CYC mentees, a high school sophomore and a recent immigrant, asked me to accompany him to schedule a dentist's appointment at the university's dental clinic. When we reached the pediatric center, two receptionists were standing behind the desk. One of the receptionists was speaking Cantonese to a mother about her child's upcoming appointment. The other receptionist, a White male, asked, "Can I help you?" As we were trying to set-up the appointment, I asked the receptionist if translation services would be available the day of the appointment. He told me, "No, we don't provide that here." When I asked, "How come translation services are available at the medical institution but not here?" the other receptionist, who was now done speaking to the mother, commented, "We are a university. We don't do that here." I asked the receptionist who spoke Cantonese, if he could help my mentee and his parents the day of the appointment, he repeated, "We don't do that here." After we exited the building, my mentee said to me, "Even though I didn't understand what you were all saying, the way they were talking was quite rude."

*****

A local theater that played new movie releases from Hong Kong was right next door to one of the strip clubs. The theater closed in the late 1980s and remained closed until the late 1990s when it was converted to a Chinese restaurant. The décor in the grand interior remains untouched today.

The theater brings back a lot of childhood memories for me. It was the late-1980s. I was about five to seven years old. Once to twice a month on the weekends, I would go to one of the early evening showings with my gor gor, parents and/or my parents' friends. As recent immigrants, going to the theater in Chinatown was one of the few entertainment outlets that my parents and my parents' friends could enjoy. At that time, I remembered feeling full of joy and extremely safe. I am not sure if it was because the adults I loved were there or it was still early; however, I do not have a clear image of the red light district at that time. As I got older, that image changed dramatically to luxurious high-rises that dominated the skyline.

*****

As urban downtowns become attractive luxurious living, Chinatowns and other working-poor communities of color across the United States have become prime real-estate zones. The luxury-housing and economic boom resulted in skyrocketing rents and costs, and such neighborhoods are experiencing the threat of gentrification. For instance, one of the recently constructed luxury condo building charges more than $4,000 a month for a one-bedroom apartment. Today, as a result of the soaring real-estate prices in the area and the Chinatown community's years of protests, most of the red light district establishments have vanished. However, there are still some establishments that are clearly visible. Unlike the previous establishments, they are more upscale and have a cleaned up image.

Chinatown is also minutes away to the Financial and the reviving Theater Districts. While the Theater District borders Chinatown, they are worlds apart. In contrast to the old theater in Chinatown, the ticket prices in this upscale district are far too expensive for many of the Chinatown residents.

> *Even though we would pass by the Theater District everyday after school, I had never seen a Broadway show until I was in graduate school. I brought my younger brother, who was thirteen at the time, to see The Lion King musical and I remember how different the exterior and interior were when compared to Chinatown, which is only a block away. An air of privilege surrounded us.*

Steps away from the Theater District stands a new YMCA ("Y"), which was opened in 2000. Before the new Y was opened, children, young people, adults, and elders in the community had very limited recreational spaces. During the 1980s and 1990s, some young people might hang out and play sports at the old Y, which was supposed to be a temporary structure. The university promised the Chinatown community that they would provide a new Y in exchange of their drastic takeover of the community's land. However, what was meant to be two to four years turned into forty plus years. There was no heat, leaky roofs, and extremely small. Others would hang out at Hope School's gym or on the streets "because there wasn't really a place to hangout," recalled Susan, "or if you weren't in athletics … then you were there to watch people and just hangout, because there wasn't really a place to hangout."

Several bus and subway station stops are in or near Chinatown. One of the subway stations is located right below the medical institution. As long as I can remember this subway station always existed. In the 1990s, with housing and business development occurring in the area, a second station was opened. It is located where the red light district once stood. Today, the area is the site of multiple recently built luxury condos and hotels, which are all in a one- to four-block radius. As a result of the high cost of living, many residents end up displaced as they are forced and have no choice but move miles away from friends, community, and jobs into suburbs and cities that are outside of Harborview. While some of these communities are accessible through public transportation, others are not.

Additionally, Chinatown is a few blocks away from the Brick Hill neighborhood and the downtown area with major department stores and various smaller shops.

Woolworth's and other major department stores in downtown were places my mommie would take my gor gor and me on most of the weekends. My gor gor and I could spend the entire day inside Woolworth's, especially the toy's section. My gor gor and I both knew we were only allowed to look, play some of the toys, and read some of the children's books in the store. But that was fine with us. Happiness filled our young minds. Being able to go on our downtown adventures with mommie was all we craved, because Saturdays meant it was her day off. Today, the sites of my childhood adventures are quickly vanishing. Woolworth's and two prominent department stores have long been closed or sold. One news reporter recently noted, the new mixed-use towers that are under construction would "transform downtown forever."

*****

Although Chinatown is just a few blocks away from Brick Hill they are worlds apart. Brick Hill is home to upper middle class and upper class individuals and families, most of whom are politicians and professionals, while the majority of the residents in Chinatown prior to the developments were immigrants and working poor to low income people.

The chronic traffic congestions in Chinatown, as a result of the commuters working in the area, evening theater-goers, shoppers, tourists, restaurant-goers, unhoused individuals, paramedics heading to the hospital, construction workers building luxury condos, and late-night drug dealers and prostitutes, occurs seven days a week and practically 24 hours a day. The interstate highways, medical institutions, the adult entertainment district, and the development of luxurious condos and hotels are some of the great reminders of how Harborview's Chinatown, like many low-income communities and communities of color, has been affected by urban renewal, gentrification, capitalism, and institutional racism. Jeff, a CYC Youth Worker, explains as a result of the income and wealth disparities, the voices of low-income and immigrant communities are very often silenced in society:

There are certain communities that have more voice because of economic means, because of block voting and political connection. And of course, "you're an immigrant, who cares about you?" Immigrants do not have voting power because they cannot vote until they are citizens. Even when they can vote, there's other issues that affects their right to vote.

Here are some personal reflections about Harborview's Chinatown written by my college students,[2] when we visited Chinatown in August 2007. These reflections represent what most individuals, who are not familiar with Chinatown, observe from an educational visit to "Chinatown":

... when one looks around Chinatown the major focal points are the stores and the bright signs. I would have never thought that there are actually people who live above and around the stores.

—A WHITE STUDENT

[The fieldtrip provided] a firsthand look of how big business are slowly taking over Chinatown and turning Chinatown into a business venture. Like many immigrants or minorities, Asians are feeling the brunt of capitalism. I think it's a collective effort by the white power structure that does not want any change. This white power structure wants to keep things the same and does not want to see Asians or any other minority group to rise up.

—A HAITIAN AMERICAN STUDENT

Chinatown is so crowded and yet there are still many families lived there. I can't believe the lack of space and how narrow the alleys are. I didn't realize that before.

—A VIETNAMESE AMERICAN STUDENT

One thing I learned was that Chinatown was full of so many memories, good and bad. When you told us about the highway system they built through Chinatown, I thought to myself, 'Wow, I thought that highways always existed in Chinatown.' I thought it was one of Chinatown's earliest structures. Chinatown was so diverse ... When I looked through restaurant windows, I saw families sit together, conversing and having a good time. I felt the importance of family.

—A NIGERIAN AMERICAN STUDENT

The above quotes illustrate the multilayers and perspectives of Chinatowns, particularly from those who are not connected and familiar with such space and place. The first and third quotes comment on the physical structure of Chinatown, while the third and fourth quotes engage historical, political, and social aspects.

The following four reflections are from students who have a personal connection with Chinatown:

I go to Chinatown at least once a week for food and to do errands. However, I had never realized that there's a lot of history lies on these small streets of Chinatown. When people talk about Chinatown they only think of food and restaurants. But there is residential area where people live.

—A CHINESE AMERICAN STUDENT

Even though this is the east coast, people do not complain of racism, I believe that it still exists here. [Harborview], overall, has a history of subtle racism which can be seen to match the strength of much which has been seen out west. Whether it be the [red-light district] during the eighties or the construction of the major highway through Chinatown, the state government has cared little for this particular community. It continues to slowly take away the community until there may be nothing left. The fact that many of the people living here are slowly being evicted out of the historical site means something is going on in the shadows.

—A HAPA[3] STUDENT

One of the major reasons I did not enjoy going to Chinatown was because of the bad smells. The streets are dirty. There is never trash on [the Brick Hill neighborhood, which is steps away from Chinatown]. It just shows the government only cares about themselves, not [the] minority group. Living in a dirty filthy environment cannot be good for the community's moral.

—A CHINESE AMERICAN STUDENT

Chinatown is not only a place for us to visit, but it has become a part of our daily lives.

—A CHINESE AMERICAN STUDENT

The above reflections amplify the realities of those who live and are a part of Chinatown. The second and third quotes highlight the long-lasting impact of institutional racism. The first and fourth quotes remind us that Chinatowns have always been a home and community for individuals and families.

*****

Harborview Chinatown Community Center

HCCC aims to improve the lives of Harborview's Asian American community through bridging the dominant cultural norms *and* honoring the community's cultural wealth. HCCC is centrally located in the community and provides a wide range of services, thus making it very accessible. While a diverse population utilizes HCCC's services, Chinese immigrant families are the prime group at the CBO. HCCC's funding source and support comes from various entities, with governmental (35–45%) and foundation grants (20–22%) making up over half of their revenue. Today, after more than forty-five years in the community, HCCC offers the community eight programs. CYC is one of eight programs that the HCCC offers to Harborview's Asian American community.

During a school building boom that occurred throughout Harborview in the 1970s, local residents in Chinatown and two neighboring communities formed HCCC because they wanted input in the design of a new school in Chinatown. Susan explained:

There's this huge [school] institution coming into the community that is going to be closed for half the day. So there was a movement not just in Chinatown, but throughout the city, because there are other schools like this in other neighborhoods of [Harborview]. So there's a movement in [Harborview] to make these facilities available to the community when the schools are not in session.

Within each new school, the city specifically designed space for a community school partnership because in the 1970s, community involvement became a central issue in school reform, especially in communities that have been traditionally underserved (Epstein & Sanders, 2000). Susan described that throughout Harborview "there was an effort to move away from the brick schoolhouses to these large multi-use complexes that in theory are suppose to be one-stop shops for government and schools ... so the [Hope Elementary] School was part of that movement." After the completion of Hope Elementary School in the late 1970s, Harborview designated HCCC to run the community school program because "the residents wanted to get a group of people from the community just to start making decisions in and for the school [and] to welcome more Asian American students" (Wai-Ming, past Director of CYC, personal interview, January 2005). Susan similarly added:

> ... [P]eople who lived in the community wanted to be able to say "Well if this is suppose to be a community school then the community needs to have an input into the school, into the process, and to have a voice when the school was being designed and built". And that's how [HCCC] started. We were the community piece of it. And it wasn't just Chinatown. It was residents from Chinatown [and two neighboring communities] ... Because the school sits on the cusp of 3 neighborhoods so the people who were involved with the planning process represented those areas. It wasn't just Asians. There were Latinos. There were African Americans. There were Whites. You know, to make sure the community had access and that they had their needs addressed ... And from the stories that I hear is that meetings would be packed and there would just be a lot of people attending even though they were not on the board. There were a lot of residents. You know people who were invested in the process would come out.

In 1969, HCCC was able to obtain a lease from the city to operate one of the old abandoned warehouses that had become eminent domains. The different sites later became a major battle ground between the different nonprofit CBOs in Chinatown (HCCC was one of them), the city, and the medical institution, as a result of a redevelopment project agreement, which I call Chinatown Development Project (CDP).

HCCC's programs

Today, after more than forty-five years in the community, HCCC offers a variety of services that aim to enrich and improve Asian Americans in the Harborview area. HCCC serves over 4,000 children, youth, and adults each year. When developing programs, Susan noted the importance of understanding what the community's needs are in order to be responsive: "If you develop programs that don't address any of the needs then there's no point. You're not really creating something that helps the people that you are trying to serve." The eight programs that HCCC offers to the community include: (1) early childcare; (2) adult education; (3) year-round afterschool for 5–13 year olds; (4) year-round youth center for 11–20 year olds (i.e., CYC); (5) family-based toddler and infant care; (6) recreation; (7) family service and support; and (8) art and culture center for children, youth, and adults.

The Early Childcare program was HCCC's first program, which started as a bilingual playgroup in the early 1970s and then two years later the program opened. It is the first bilingual (Chinese and English) childcare program in the State. They serve ages 1.5 to 6 years old. They have about 81 slots available. For twenty-seven years, the early childcare program had been housed at On-Ping Village and HCCC's old building site until 2005 when HCCC opened its new building. The Adult Education program started when Hope Elementary School opened in 1976 with two part-time staffs. It now offers several levels of ESL classes for adults as well as bilingual citizenship classes and advocacy and counseling services. Susan explained why these two programs were and remain among the most vital for the community:

> [O]ur core constituency was immigrants. And what are the most basic services? Child-care and English. People need to work and learn English and somebody to watch their kids, that's why those are the most pressing needs. You can ask any parent, what is the most challenging thing you deal with as parents and a lot of it is childcare because without childcare, you can't work.

In the same year, the Recreation program started with the gym and pool usage at Hope Elementary School.

Later, in order to meet the community needs HCCC started adding other programs. The year-round Afterschool program, open to 5–13 year olds, is housed in the ground level of Hope Elementary School. The program and Hope Elementary School are partners. As one of Harborview's largest after school programs, it serves 130 to 160 school-age young children year-round. Both the early childcare and year-round afterschool programs have a waitlist. The Family-based Toddler and Infant Care program, a home-based program with 36 available openings, was started in the mid-1990s because the Early Childcare program was growing and thus unable to manage infants. Additionally, "there isn't a lot of affordable infant care anywhere," noted Susan. "Infant care is expensive everywhere. And if you need bilingual infant care, it's even harder. I mean there wasn't that many in Chinatown before." The program also helps train Chinese women so that "they can provide safe care and licensed childcare." HCCC helps and supports the women in getting their Child Development Associate certificate and their Associate's Degree in Early Childhood Education. Susan explained in detail:

We train these women and we maintain their contracts and licenses for them with the State. We don't hire them. It's a small business enterprise. We're kind of a bridge. We do the trainings. We do the support. It's really helping women to start their own business [out of their own homes] and to learn the skills, not to be just babysitters but to provide early education because the kids go directly to school or they go directly to our the early childcare program ... it's a way to address the need for infant and toddler care in the community but it's also making sure there's quality care.

HCCC is the only Chinese speaking family childcare network in the state, as Susan asserted:

> We're the only one of its kind. There's no other Chinese-speaking family childcare network. There's about 50 providers and we've trained all of them—every woman who is a family childcare provider who is Chinese.

Not surprisingly, there are children who have participated in all four of HCCC services, which Susan describes as "kind of a natural ladder."

The Family Support program started in 2005 with a coordinator who is a Licensed Independent Clinical Social Worker and has about twenty-five active cases. Even though this is a new program, family support services have been a component of HCCC for ten years where it used to be in each of HCCC's programs. After trying several different models, HCCC decided to have the Family Support as its own separate program because the programs were replicating services for the same families. Susan explained in detail why HCCC created the separate program:

> When you have someone coordinating as a whole, then you're able to identify crossovers and then you're able to be more effective on how you work with families because you can work with the youth and at the same time the toddler and the parent in adult education. We also wanted to provide services, and we realize that we needed to do this more than just the parent in our programs. We needed to do this for the community as a whole.

According to Susan, family support was always something that the previous Executive Director (ED), who was the ED for more than fifteen years, wanted to strengthen in the community:

> It's critical to the community because if you're not looking at the family as a whole, you're not really helping anybody. You're helping individuals but you're not helping the whole cohort move forward ... It's the entire family unit. Unless you can really go to the root of what is causing the issues, you're going to keep going on the same cycle of intervention and prevention. You're not going to really move them out of that cycle.

While there are some programs that shame parents and families and devalues their culture or their perspective on parenting, HCCC's "goal is not to change parents." Susan elaborated:

> The goal is not to change parents [rather] the goal is to educate them because you can't change somebody ... You look at what the strengths are and you move from there. So when [the Family Support Coordinator] works with families, [this person] doesn't shame them or tell them what they are doing wrong. [The coordinator] starts from what they are doing right and then you start building in suggestions of how you can even make that stronger or better. When you come from that asset based approach, you don't turn off people because you recognize their strengths.

HCCC remains one of the largest Asian American nonprofit community-based organizations and a multiservice provider in the East Coast. The staffs' passion and commitment are clearly visible in the community. "There's a lot of honesty about the work that you're doing at HCCC," explained Rachel, who as the new Director of CYC immediately noticed the organization's holistic approach and dynamics. "It's not about working for HCCC, but it's really about working for the community."

"You're fighting a garage": HCCC's struggles in finding a "home"

Until 2005, when HCCC opened its new building, their programs and administration offices were housed in six rented spaces throughout Chinatown. Susan noted that being dispersed into six different sites did not give HCCC a lot of stability, because "being in downtown Harborview we didn't control the real estate market ... Our leases have to be renegotiated every 2 years." One of the rented sites, which was the original home for some of the programs including CYC, was purchased by HCCC from the city prior to the Chinatown Development Plan (CDP).

In the 1950s and 1960s, Harborview took over empty buildings, which included the ones that were part of the CDP, as a result of urban renewal. Throughout the 1980s and 1990s, the medical institution, which has already taken up many of the land in Chinatown, proposed to build a large parking garage on the site. On several occasions, "the developers paid young people to go out and do outreach ... and advocacy" around Chinatown and some of the youth from CYC were approached by the developers, noted Jeff, a Youth Worker at CYC. After twenty plus years of protest and "three different attempts" made by the medical institution in trying to build a parking garage (phone conversation with a community organizer, April 28, 2005), the community finally defeated a proposal for a parking garage on the site in 1994. "If the community didn't get the CDP it would've impacted everybody, not just HCCC," said Susan, "because it would've changed this community ... you're fighting a garage."

The city worked with the local community to develop an alternative plan where a series of sponsored bilingual community meetings were held to discuss and plan what should be built on CDP. Susan mentioned, "Part of the negotiation was that there should be some community benefit from this development, so that there's space for organizations." The final plan included a 23-story high rise with ground-floor retail, elderly housing, commercial and community program space, two levels of underground parking, and 251 units of housing, 115 (or 46%) of which will be affordable. Moreover, the city's mayor signed an agreement that preserved CDP for housing and would forbid all institutional use on the land. Since HCCC owned their portion of the CDP, they either had to tear their building down or the CDP had to build around them. The board of directors decided to tear the building down and "swap the building and lots for a new building," explained Susan, because "it was a horrible building" where "the floors were crooked and the systems were antiquated ... The building wasn't operational." Some of the youth who started coming to CYC when they were at the old site recalled similar images: "the building was so old," "We imagined that one day it would fall down," or "It was always dark ... It was so scary walking up to the second floor." The building was demolished in the summer of 2002 and the new structure was completed during the summer of 2004.

HCCC's new community center has five stories and 20,000 square feet, including multipurpose classrooms, a computer center, playground, and a rooftop garden to house their current programs and allow room for future programming. The new building is also a green building, which Susan developed and led. When I asked Susan why having a green building is important for HCCC, she explained the importance of respecting and honoring the people and community that you serve:

> It goes back to what the community deserves. Having a green building is efficient so we're efficient with energy and water usage. But it's also important for the people who use the building. We have people who are in this building for 10 hours a day and children are here for 10 hours a day. When you have a green building, it means they are not inhaling toxins, your quality is pure. There's better air in here then there's outside. We also live in Chinatown, which is smog filled and has extremely high asthma rates. So having a green building is just another way of respecting your community and also conserving the environment and resources.

When the new and permanent building opened, HCCC was able to focus on the internal system and doing strategic planning because "we had programs that never knew each other before we moved into this building. And part of this operational inward reflection is going to be strategic planning process, too," commented Susan.

Everyone at HCCC is extremely excited to have all of the programs housed at the new community center and at Hope Elementary School instead of being scattered in six different sites. Moreover, in 2014, HCCC celebrated the grand opening in a city located directly south of Harborview and with a substantial Asian American population. As a result of gentrification and urban renewal in Harborview, many Asian Americans began moving and settling here.

Community Youth Center

Opened in 1995, CYC works with youth ages 11–20 of which over 80 percent qualify for free or reduced lunches. CYC was formed with the idea of serving middle and high school youth living or hanging out in Chinatown because the HCCC realized there were limited youth programs in the community. Susan, who was the first CYC director, was hired in the early 1990s to start the youth program. In developing the youth program, Susan did a lot of reading as well as visiting different youth programs in Harborview. She reflected on the process:

> I was given a lot of freedom [by everyone at HCCC] to learn because I was learning on the job ... The field of youth work was fairly new to me. So I was given a lot of flexibility and support to learn it and to experiment with it. So the first few years, you know, I thought it would take me 3–5 years to get the program running. But it really took 3 to 5 years to figure out what a youth program for this community should look like. And what the needs should be that we address.

From the very beginning, Susan firmly believed in addressing social justice and community issues in CYC. She explained:

> I was really passionate about justice issues. You know social justice, equality, opportunity and the whole racial discourse. So that's kinda how we were talking and [the assistant director at the time] put it in context of working with young people and really providing the means to shape their opportunities ... I also had a firm belief that we address the needs of both American born as well as the immigrant youth because we're a community that encompasses both. In order to be an effective service deliverer for your community, you need to address the polarity within the community, because the needs are so different. But at the same time, provide opportunities for those two completely different groups to come together and have meaningful discourse and relationships. And that was the basis of CYC's Youth Leadership and Mentorship program.

CYC aims to develop the academic, social, emotional, and leadership skills of Asian American youth and engage young people with their family, school, and community. It offers college preparatory and ESL classes, volunteer-run academic tutoring, social recreational activities, and leadership skills building since "these all build very necessary skills in young people," expressed Susan.

While Susan created the core programs at CYC, she "want[ed] people to have freedom with it," explained Susan. "You know, [Wai-Ming, the previous Director of CYC] had freedom to change things. The only thing I tell the program director is the fact they need to always have those three cores of programming." Susan also recollected the field of youth work, when youth programming was relatively new a decade ago:

> A lot of the focus was just on getting kids off the street. Occupying them with whatever, giving them a ball. You know, that was never my intention what the youth program was. You have to give them more than a ball. You can give them a ball, but what else are you going to do with them. You are going to teach them how to play ball, but you have to teach them how they can interact with each other, how they create meaningful dialogue between each other and things like that.

CYC's academic programs

> ESL classes are targeted for a lot of the new immigrants—most of them are recent immigrants and occasionally we have some ABC [American-born Chinese]. It's to help them improve in their English with the hope they would transition in school better and understand more. We also have the tutoring program and some of them are not able to do their homework independently so hopefully through that we can help them out. There are also preparation classes. A lot of them might not have the experience of test taking. These kinds of test preparation classes would provide them with more knowledge.
>
> —Cindy, Tutoring Coordinator

Cindy provided a glimpse into the three academic support units that CYC offers: English as a Second Language (ESL) classes, tutoring program, and test preparation classes and college access series.

"Completely volunteer-run": The tutoring program and test preparation classes

The tutoring program runs on Mondays and Wednesdays for two hours each day and, as Cindy, the Tutor Coordinator, mentioned, "It's completely volunteer-run." In terms of recruitment outreach, Cindy explained that CYC is registered on several nonprofit websites and she also sends out "a bunch of fliers" to the local colleges and universities and other local nonprofits. While there are a few who respond to the fliers, the majority of the tutors are high school and college students who were former tutees at CYC. The main objective of the tutoring program is to improve the academic and social well-being of the youth. Through interactions with the youth, the staff members notice the youths' academic and social well-being needed to be served. CYC takes the time to match up the tutors and tutees. Cindy explains:

> We do look at their grades in order to match the student. If the student needs help in ... algebra we're going to, of course, match up someone who is really good in algebra. All of the tutors need to go through an interview. During the interview, I ask the tutors what subject areas are they comfortable in teaching and if they feel comfortable working with high school or middle school students, female or male. They have to submit proof to us that they are doing well in that academic area by giving us a copy of their previous year's report card. And it's ongoing that we ask our volunteers to submit their report cards. We want to make sure they are doing well in that area.

In order to be a tutor, Cindy noted, "They need to have consistently good grades" because "if they are going to be teaching a student, they are going to be a role model." CYC's approach to the tutoring program is what Noam, Biancarosa, and Dechausay (2003) describe as "homework as an opportunity to build relationships and target tutoring" where the program is also seen as a mentoring opportunity (p. 40). For instance, the tutors keep track of their tutees' progress through weekly evaluations and then Cindy meets with the tutors every month and "within that meeting we talk about all of the students' improvements and needs." Additionally, CYC began offering test preparation classes about two to three years ago because the staffs "noticed there was population of students," Cindy stated, "that needed extra help so we started doing preparation classes. We started with the [elite public high school entrance exam] and then later we added other classes like SATs, [the state mandated exam], TOEFL." Similar to the tutoring program, the preparation classes are volunteer-run as well. High school juniors or seniors and college students, who have been through the process, often run the classes. With the many colleges and universities in the area, CYC outreaches to them or often receives a few requests from college students to volunteer their time.

In using a contextually *and* culturally sensitive approach in serving the community, CYC understands the youths' family situations and thus creates alternative forms of serving, communicating, and connecting with parents about their children's academic progress. For instance, knowing that the majority of the parents have long work schedules (i.e., contextually sensitive approach), Cindy mails progress reports once a month to parents and often makes follow-up phone calls. She explained, "even though we might not have a chance to talk to the parents, at least they know what's going on." CYC acknowledges and is sensitive to the youths' family background and circumstances, and finds alternative ways to communicate with parents. Additionally, all of CYC's materials (e.g., schedules, forms, and brochures) are in English and Chinese (i.e., culturally sensitive approach). As a result, parents learn (more) about CYC's programming and what their children are doing, which gives them the opportunity to feel connected and be a part of the social network. Youth also feel welcome since they see their culture appreciated and, as in the case of recent immigrants, hear their home language spoken (i.e., contextually and culturally sensitive approach).

The significance of the "one-on-one relationship": The ESL classes

The three ESL classes have about twelve students enrolled in each class during the school year and twenty-five students is the maximum in the summer. The classes are scheduled for twice a week for an hour each time during the school year. Erin, the ESL coordinator, described the importance of having small class sizes and a contextual approach:

> I don't like them too large. With ESL classes, that's how I was trained to become an ESL teacher … I don't believe in just filling a room with people just fill it up. I believe in quality time so I don't want to take more than 10 youth in each class … there's more opportunities for them to get one-on-one time. If they don't know something, they'll ask me. It's small so they could get it explained. We play a lot more games. It's a smaller group so there's more practice for each one of them to speak or to repeat a word.

Wai-Ming, CYC previous director, explained why she, too, emphasized the one-on-one class size setting:

> I don't want it to be like school. I always tell [the ESL coordinator] that … I want to make it different … And with one-on-one, [the ESL coordinator] will be able to really retain and build the relationship and that will come through when she has more time with the students … I don't want it to be like school where you have 40 youth. And then that's it, you lose that relationship and why bother coming. So I do value that.

The youth also noted small class sizes, culturally sensitive staffs and materials were what made the ESL classes and CYC as a whole significant, and thus different from their schools. Betty, a sixth grade at the time of this research, is one of the youth who regularly attended CYC's ESL classes. She found the ESL classes valuable because it "teaches us the 'cultural differences' between Chinese and American culture." For instance, Betty remembered in one of the class, the topic was comparing Chinese and U.S. American weddings. She noted the difference between the two cultures is the clothing colors: "In Chinese culture, people like to wear red on their wedding day but Americans only like to wear white and black. These colors represent death for us." The lesson provided an opportunity for Betty and other recent immigrant youth to understand U.S. American culture, in this case, wedding traditions. These topics are important because some of these lessons and discussions are often assumed knowledge for people or they are held accountable for knowing these rules that no one has taught them (Delpit, 1988, 1995).

Betty also remembered reading a short article about an immigrant student feeling uncomfortable participating in school. Betty explained how she related with the student:

> I feel like I am that student because I do the same thing in school. I never raise my hand in class because I am scared that I would get the words wrong, like I would mispronounce the words. I am more comfortable and confident talking during CYC's ESL class because it's smaller and I know the people.

The youth commented the large class size at school affected their learning. For instance, comments such as "there are too many students in the class" and "the teachers at school are unable to give everyone individual attention" were frequently repeated. Other scholars, such as Rubinstein-Ávila (2006), also noted the importance of the one-on-one focus in OST spaces since many of the youth attended overcrowded schools. At the same time, the youth appreciated how the OST staffs "*show* you how" and "don't just assume" you already know the materials (p. 267). CYC offers additional English assistance for youth that the schools are unable to provide due to the increase in standardized testing, large class sizes, and culturally insensitive schools. Equally important, the rise of anti-immigrant sentiments and antibilingual initiatives in our schools across the nation has placed English language learners and children of immigrants with limited resources and, essentially, in the margins. As a result, the youth feel most comfortable in expressing themselves at CYC.

In addition to the academic services, the center runs many clubs, which change every two to three months. The clubs are "based on interest and is based on what the youth want," noted Erin, CYC's ESL teacher. For example, toward the end of the summer, I recalled the staffs would ask the youth to fill out a survey of what clubs interest them and based on the response the staff members designed various areas: cooking, band, yoga, crafting, comic books, and hip-hop dancing clubs. Older youth who are in high school are able to develop their leadership skills either through CYC's year-long Youth Leadership and Mentorship program or their year-long Business program. The leadership and mentorship program offers 15–20 high school young people opportunities to develop workshops and activities for their peers and serve as role models for the younger teens (i.e., middle school age youth) at the center. At the same time, while there are structured classes and clubs that require enrollment, CYC also runs unstructured activities. For instance, during "floor time," youth and staff members would play video, board and card games (e.g., Uno, Risk and Monopoly), ping-pong, gym time, computer games, sing karaoke, or engage in dialogue. The "free choice" design encourages young people to manage their schedule, which Susan noted is an important skill:

> For a program like ours where we would want to encourage choice because that's part of the skill set that youths need to gain is to manage their choices and how to carry through their obligations. I think youths come because they choose to come and they stay because they choose to stay.

The importance of choice at CYC illustrates how young people have a say in their development.

Today, besides serving young people from Chinatown, youth from and beyond Harborview come to CYC. During the years that I was at CYC, membership cost was $35 per year for youth who are 13 and over and $25 per year for youth who are 11–12. Today, they have eliminated membership cost to make programs more accessible to all youth. Instead, there is a small fee for the academic and summer programs. The low cost is an important factor for the youth and families. Additionally, the community views CYC as a good quality and safe place for young people during out-of-school hours. One youth explained:

> Before CYC, I participated in a tutoring program near Chinatown. It was actually quite pricey for my family's income. My mom feel we need to go to these tutoring classes, because our English is not up to the level of other kids in our grade are supposed to be. So she feels responsible to pay for these expenses to let us improve our English; but the program was just too costly. When I heard about CYC and the low cost of the different programs and activities that they offer, I was really excited. It definitely helped. In that aspect, participating in CYC helped with my family expenses. It's a place that my mom knows I am in a safe place after school. Or else, I would just be going home and struggling with homework by myself.

CYC's hours of operation take into account the parents' work hours because CYC understands the majority of the parents' schedules. CYC is open from Mondays through Fridays from 2 p.m. to 7 p.m., except during Daylight Saving Time when it closes at 6:30 p.m. from Mondays through Thursdays and at 7 p.m. on Fridays. At the time of this research, CYC began to offer weekend hours as well. Thirty-five to 50 youth fill the space daily during the school year while over 50 youth attend each day during the summer months. CYC's summer program offers low-cost morning ESL classes and afternoon enrichment activities and field trips.

This chapter served as a contextual history of Chinatowns, Harborview, and HCCC. In the following chapter, I discuss in depth the parents' work and family situations along with their experiences with their children's schools. These experiences are crucial in order for educators, practitioners, and policy makers to better understand and serve low-income Chinese and Asian American youth and their families. Without knowing and acknowledging their personal and family experiences, we are ignoring and silencing their experiences and needs.

Notes

1. Chinese merchants, students, scholars, and government officials were exempted from the Exclusion Act.
2. Summer of 2007, I taught an undergraduate Asian American Studies course at the local four-year public university. For our last day of classes, I took my students on a Chinatown fieldtrip and these were some of their personal reflections of the experience. The fieldtrip was adapted from Dr. Peter Kiang's curriculum.
3. Hapa is a Hawai'ian term meaning "half" and "of mixed descent." Today, the term generally refers to people of mixed-Asian and/or Pacific Islander ancestry.

Works cited

Chu, L. M. (1974). *The images of China and the Chinese in the Overland Monthly, 1868–1875, 1883–1935*. San Francisco, CA: R and E Research Associates.

Delpit, L. (1988). The silenced dialogue: Power and pedagogy in educating other people's children. *Harvard Educational Review, 58*(3), 280–298.

Delpit, L. (1995). *Other people's children: Cultural conflict in the classroom*. New York, NY: The New Press.

Epstein, J. L., & Sanders, M. G. (2000). Connecting home, school, and community: New directions for social research. In M. T. Hallinan (Ed.), *Handbook of the sociology of education* (pp. 285–306). New York, NY: Kluwer Academic/Plenum Publishers.

Glenn, E. N. (1985). Racial ethnic women's labor: The intersection of race, gender and class oppression. *Review of Radical Political Economics, 17*(3), 86–108.

Kwong, P. (1979). *Chinatown, N.Y.: Labor & politics, 1930–1950*. New York, NY: Monthly Review Press.

Kwong, P. (1987). *The new Chinatown*. New York, NY: Hill and Wang.

Kwong, P. (1997). *Forbidden workers: Illegal Chinese immigrants and American labor*. New York, NY: The New Press.

Loo, C. M. (1991). *Chinatown: Most time, hard time*. New York, NY: Praeger Publishers.

Noam, G. G., Biancarosa, G., & Dechausay, N. (2003). *Afterschool education: Approaches to an emerging field*. Cambridge, MA: Harvard Education Press.

Older, D. J. (2014, April 8). Gentrification's insidious violence: The truth about American cities. *Salon*. Retrieved from http://www.salon.com/2014/04/08/gentrification

Rubinstein-Ávila, E. (2006). Publishing "Equinox": An ethnographic tale of youth literacy development after school. *Anthropology & Education Quarterly, 37*(3), 255–272.

Sung, B. L. (1972). *The Chinese in America*. New York, NY: The Macmillan Company.

Sung, B. L. (1987). *The adjustment experiences of Chinese immigrant children in New York City*. New York, NY: Center for Migration Studies.

To, W. K., & The Chinese Historical Society of New England. (2008). *Images of American: Chinese in Boston 1870–1965*. Charleston, SC: Arcadia Publishing.

Wong, M. G. (2006). Chinese Americans. In P. G. Min (Ed.), *Asian Americans: Contemporary trends and issues* (2nd ed., pp. 110–145). Thousand Oaks, CA: Pine Forge Press.

Wu, E. D. (2014, January 23). Asian American and the 'model minority' myth. *Los Angeles Times*. Op-Ed. Retrieved from http://www.latimes.com/opinion/op-ed/la-oe-0123-wu-chua-model-minority-chinese-20140123-story.html

Yuan, D. Y. (1963). Voluntary segregation: A study of new Chinatown. *Phylon, 24*(3), 255–265.

Yung, J., & The Chinese Historical Society of America. (2006). *Images of American: San Francisco's Chinatown*. Charleston, SC: Arcadia Publishing.

Zhou, M. (1992). *Chinatown: The socioeconomic potential of an urban enclave*. Philadelphia, PA: Temple University Press.

CHAPTER THREE

Parents' relationship with children and U.S. schools

I didn't know anything about the U.S. school system ... When my oldest son started school, I was absolutely confused and unaware of how things worked. I felt the whole process was extremely intimidating. The difficulty of not knowing anyone was very challenging. I didn't have any of my family in the U.S. I had no support network here. I did not have anyone to ask for help. Additionally, I didn't have time to attend school events because I needed to work. If I had the time, of course, I would have attended the school events, but I just did not. The language barrier was also a problem for me. My English wasn't good and no one spoke Cantonese at the school. To be honest, I wasn't able to attend many of the school meetings and events.

—MS. CHAN, PARENT

It's like all of the blame gets placed on parents because they are working poor parents, but there's so little communication between the school and the parents. So imagine immigrant parents who don't speak English and the kid don't speak English, how do you really make that transition for them to acculturate to the whole school culture? How do schools communicate with parents?

—JEFF, CYC YOUTH WORKER[1]

Researchers have painted vivid and powerful stories of post-1965 immigrant parents and families[2] in the United States, especially about their immigration experiences, life in the U.S. such as living and work conditions, and children's schooling. For example, see Delgado-Gaitan (2004); Kibria (1993); Ong (2003); Portes and Rumbaut (2001); Suárez-Orozco and Suárez-Orozco (2001); Valdés (1996); What Kids Can Do (2006). Like those stories, Ms. Chan and Jeff both provided a glimpse of the dilemmas that low-income immigrant families often encounter on a daily basis with their children's schooling in the United States. Similar to other research (Adler, 2007; Delgado-Gaitan, 2004; Ji & Koblinsky, 2009; Li, 2010; Suárez-Orozco & Suárez-Orozco, 2001; Valdés, 1996), my research showed that low-income and working poor immigrant parents do value education and are supportive of their children. However, parents are too often unable to navigate and negotiate within U.S. school contexts. Parents' limited understanding of the U.S. education system and schools' lack of culturally relevant and multilingual services are obstacles for them. The parents' jobs frequently require them to work extensive hours, further limiting opportunities for interaction with schools and other institutions. For instance, Adler (2007) found in her research on Hmong home–school relations that parents "often have difficulty participating in the schools due to linguistic differences, conflicting work schedules, and a sense of role separation between school and home responsibilities" (p. 85). This is a vicious and demoralizing cycle. As I (2013) explained, parents have limited access to employment because of language barriers and a continued language barrier due to the rigid nature of their jobs, thus they are unable to negotiate and legitimately participate in schools serving their children (e.g., Adler, 2007; Collingnon, Men, & Tan, 2001; Ji & Koblinsky, 2009; Siu, 2002; Wong, 2010, 2011, 2013). Furthermore, low-income and working poor immigrant families frequently struggle with negotiating the U.S. school system (Adler, 2007; Hune & Takeuchi, 2008; Lee & Kumashiro, 2005; Lew, 2006; Wong, 2013) since schools routinely have limited knowledge of (immigrant) families of color's "multiple worlds" (Phelan, Davidson, & Yu, 1998) and as a result, their "funds of knowledge" (González et al., 1995; González, Moll, & Amanti, 2005) are not seen as assets and thus are left not acknowledged. For instance, as I will illustrate, parents frequently were unaware of how the U.S. school system worked as well as their rights as parents, and essentially, a sense of separation between their family and children's schools occurs. Schools are inaccessible and restrictive institutional spaces for low-income and working poor immigrant families.

Family separation: The impact of immigration

Many of the families were separated during some point in their lives due to immigration and work. Scholars such as Qin (2006) and Suárez-Orozco and Suárez-Orozco (2001) have similarly noted the separation of one or more parent(s) was a common reality for children of immigrants and their families. As a result, "family reunification is a long, painful, and disorienting ordeal" for many children of immigrants (Suárez-Orozco & Suárez-Orozco, 2001, p. 66). For instance, Mrs. Mui and her thirteen-year-old daughter, Betty, explain the difficult and traumatic shift that the entire family unit underwent when Mrs. Mui was separated from the family. Mrs. Mui, who was a middle school teacher and later an accountant in Guangdong Province, came to the United States in 2000, and it was not until five years later when she was reunited with her husband and Betty.

> *I came to the U.S. in 2000 when my parents sponsored me. Then my husband and my daughter [Betty] came in 2005. During the five years that I was in the U.S., I lived with my parents and sister in a tiny apartment in Chinatown. I worked full-time at a donut factory, where my hours were from 4 p.m. to midnight. I would take the local bus to and from work. On the weekends and during the holidays, I worked part-time pushing dim sum carts at a restaurant in Chinatown. The pay was $40 each day. Before I went to work, I would take English classes in the mornings. On Mondays when I have a day off, I would call home. At first the long distance phone rate to China was very expensive, but then it was 10 cents per minute. During this time, I saved as much money as possible so my husband and Betty can join me in the U.S. It was really hard and stressful being separated from my husband and child for such a long time.*
> —MRS. MUI, PARENT

> *I was 6 years old when my mommy immigrated to the U.S. When she left, I lived with my daddy and paternal grandparents in China. I missed mommy a lot.*
> —BETTY, DAUGHTER

Shortly after Mr. Mui and Betty arrived in the United States, Mrs. Mui stopped working at the donut factory "because the hours wouldn't allow me to see my daughter. I would be at work when she gets home from school in the afternoons; thus, I wouldn't be able to see Betty. I wanted to spend more time with her." Around that time, Mrs. Mui found a housekeeping position at one of the world's finest hotel, which she has been working ever since. Mrs. Mui's work schedule is seasonal based. For instance, during the busy months of April to November, she often works 6 to 7 days each week and gets overtime pay. On the other hand, during the off-seasons, Mrs. Mui works 2 to 3 days each week. There is also a priority system in place where "if you've been working here for a long time, then you can request for more work hours." However, as a new employee, Mrs. Mui does not have that option.

The Muis' immigration narrative is similar to that of other families in this research. While more than half of the 1st and 1.5 generation youth immigrated to the United States as a family unit, others were separated from one or both parents for a couple of months to a few years due to immigration. Similar to other research (Qin, 2006; Suárez-Orozco & Suárez-Orozco, 2001), the separation of a family member(s) was a common reality for the young people in this research.

Ling, a sophomore in high school, was about five years old when her father came to the United States. It was not until three years later in 1988 that she, her mother, and younger brother were able to immigrate to the United States. She recalled seeing her father for the first time in three years: "I didn't remember him. When I came here I was like 'Who is this person? I don't know him.'" Even after immigrating to the United States, their family unit remains separated because Ling's father worked in another state. When I asked her how often does her dad return to Harborview, she responded "He comes back sometimes but not a lot." After staying at her uncle's apartment for a few months, the family moved into a one-bedroom apartment in Chinatown. Up until recently, Ling and her brother also did not see their mother often because of their mom's work schedule. Ling explained:

> Since my mom changed jobs, I am able to see her on weekends now; but before I didn't see her that often. Now she works Mondays to Fridays at a restaurant and she has weekends off. She leaves for work around 9ish in the morning and then doesn't come home until 10; but in the summer, it gets busy so she doesn't come home until 11 or later.

Connie, who was finishing up her first year in college, and her older sister were separated from their parents for a number of years. For instance, while in China, her father worked as a construction worker in Hong Kong while the rest of the family unit lived in Toisan. Connie's father began working in Hong Kong before she was born because there was more job opportunities and higher salary outside of Toisan at the time. Connie explains, "my dad actually went to Hong Kong after they [her parents] got married. He would travel back and visit once to twice a month." As a result, "our family was separated for a long while," explained Connie. In 1996, her father came to the United States alone through the sponsorship of his brother. Connie, her older sister, and mother remained in Toisan, because her father wanted to "provide a more stable financial income" before "bringing us over." A year later, her mother's paperwork was approved. In the end, Connie and her older sister, who was eighteen at the time, stayed with their aunt in China for almost a year before joining their parents in the United States. Connie tearfully recalled the separation from her parents: "I never really lived with my dad for long, so it wasn't really a big deal for me. But then separating with my mom is the hardest part. I was just nine when I got separated with my mom." Through all of the separations, Connie, similar to the other youth in this research, must first get reacquainted with her parents. Additionally, as Suárez-Orozco and Suárez-Orozco (2001) noted, "And when the reunification involves children who were left behind when they were young, the child will in essence be 'meeting' her [or his or their] parents" (p. 69). This was the case for Connie as well as a number of the young people.

Moreover, when the child is left for long periods with relatives, who are "neglect-ful or even abusive, there are more serious problems," especially if the child does not have a clear understanding of the immigration timeline (Suárez-Orozco & Suárez-Orozco, 2001, p. 68). As a result, the separation period often becomes "traumatic" and "stressful" for the child(ren). For instance, before Amy came to the United States at the age of eleven to be reunited with her parents, she lived with relatives in China. Amy's parents immigrated to the United States first. Her father left to the United States when she was three years old and her mother left two years later. Amy lived with her paternal grandparents and other relatives during her six to eight years of separation from her parents. Throughout this period, she experienced a great deal of verbal and physical abuse from relatives and neighbors. Amy noted, with anguish:

> Being separated from my parents was very, very sad and it scarred me a lot. Back then with domestic violence, I always experienced that. I gotten beaten by anything you can think of in this room. Everything. It's like it's not only the beating ... but it's the things that they tell me. The neighbors would tell me, 'you're an orphan, you know that? Your parents don't want you anymore.' They were adults. They would tell me that. I hear these things and I remember them. I was 5 or 6 ... My mom didn't know about this. When I came and when I told my parents about all the things that they used to do to me, my mom and I were both crying.

In general, as a result of the separation from her parents, Amy was "not close with [her] parents" during her middle and high school years, even though she expressed, "I do want to be close, but can't." When I asked her who she feels closest to, Amy responded with her friends, most of whom she met at CYC. Often immigration required one or both parents to be separated from their children.

"Paycheck to paycheck": The need to always work

Educational scholars have noted that families from working-class backgrounds are affected by a number of things in U.S. schools because they particularly struggle with negotiating the school system. For instance, Lareau (2000) argues, "social class has a powerful influence on parent involvement patterns" (p. 3). Therefore, unlike their affluent classmates', who may have the human, cultural, and social capital (Bourdieu, 1986) needed to navigate the U.S. educational system, most of the families in this research have to figure things out by themselves. Additionally, these issues and concerns that parents face are compounded by their immigrant status. Parents are unable to negotiate aspects of the school system because they lack English language skills and do not understand the U.S. educational system, which makes the process much more difficult. In addition, since the majority of the parents work in restaurants, factories, markets, and other low-paying second or third shift jobs, they are unable to attend school events.

The dilemma: Restaurant work in ethnic communities

Most of the parents work in the cleaning and food service industries, such as ethnic restaurants and supermarkets, hotel housekeeping, and garment and food distribution factories. I asked Theresa, a sophomore in high school and a second generation Chinese American, what her father does for a living, she answered:

> What does every Asian parent do? Something to do with restaurants. I have Chinese class at school and then our teacher asked 'what do your parents do?' Everyone said that their parents either owned a restaurant or one of their parents work in the kitchen. My dad is a cook.

According to Xie and Goyette (2004), the percentage of Asian Americans in cleaning and food services in 2000 was 4.7 percent (cited in Sakamoto & Xie, 2006). As a result of the insidious work hours, several parents repeated, "you need to work from day to night. By the time you get home your children are all asleep already. You really don't have time to see and talk to your children." Restaurant work offers a higher salary than other menial and/or low-paying job. The difference was $2,000 to $3,000 more per month. At the same time, many parents did not like the long hours and physical conditions associated with restaurant work because of the effects on their health and family relationships. Comments such as "restaurant work is extremely labor intensive" and "Working in restaurants will eventually take a toll on your body" were common. For instance, Mrs. Mui conveyed:

> Some people asked why my husband doesn't consider working in ethnic restaurants because the salary is higher. However, it's extremely hard work and stressful. I have occasionally expressed to my husband that it doesn't matter if our income is not as high as a restaurant salary. He would feel tired and stressed all the time … During the summer, the restaurants get extremely hot in the kitchen and then in the winter there is no "heat". I just don't want him to work in these kinds of conditions just so we could have a little more income.

Mr. Mui currently works full-time in an Asian supermarket in Harborview, where he has been working since early 2006. While the hours are similar to restaurant work, Mr. and Mrs. Mui agree, "The conditions are not as grueling."

A number of the parents have worked in restaurants but they did not like it and decided to look for other jobs. Mrs. Wong, who is in her 40s, and Joe, her only child, came to the United States in 2002 through her parents' sponsorship. Mr.

Wong remained in China and was still there at the time of this research; however, he was in the process of reuniting with his family after a separation of over eight years. Mrs. Wong was sworn in as a U.S. citizen on September 19, 2007, which she joyfully said, "I'm happy that I passed the interview. I was able to understand and answer the questions that were asked by the interviewer ... I feel my English has improved a lot. It gave me a positive feeling." At the same time, as I will show later in the chapter, obtaining citizenship does not translate into knowing how to negotiate and navigate with the dominant institutions (e.g., schools). Mrs. Wong and Joe came to the United States a few months after September 11, 2001 and Mrs. Wong remembered "the economy was bad at the time. It was really difficult to find a job anywhere." Mrs. Wong, who was now the head of the household after coming to the United States, spoke about if her husband is here with them "then the pressure wouldn't be as difficult ... Right now, I am doing everything on my own." Mrs. Wong worked two jobs when she came to the United States—a waitress at a Chinese restaurant and a helper at a hair salon—but decided the jobs were not the right fit for her because of the grueling hours. The restaurant job required her to work in the evenings and weekends and as a result, "Joe was left home alone." After nine months, Mrs. Wong decided to find another job with less grueling hours. For the past few years, she has been working as a housekeeper in a small hotel in Harborview. Although Mrs. Wong has prior work experience and qualifications in the hospitality industry in China, she noted, "I am only able to get hired in housekeeping in the U.S." Similarly, Mr. Cheung, Steven's father, worked part-time at a Chinese restaurant when he and his family arrived in the United States but stopped after about five months because of the strenuous schedule and conditions. Mrs. Cheung explained:

> My husband worked part-time in restaurants when we came to [Harborview] in 1992. He would need to work in the evenings and/or mornings. His schedule was never set. My husband didn't like this kind of lifestyle. We know you can earn more working in restaurants, but the hours are too demanding. When he found out there was a job opening at an Asian supermarket, my husband applied and has been working there ever since.

A few of the young people shared similar sentiments about their parents' work situations. Bebe, a sophomore in high school, tearfully expressed that her parents' work conditions in the United States are overwhelmingly labor intensive when compared to their life in China:

> My parents' jobs in China were pretty "relaxed." My dad worked in an office setting. He was a youth worker. He had more "free time" in China. However, it is different in the U.S. because the jobs are extremely labor intensive. People see him as worthless and

cheap because he does restaurant work. My dad would get yelled at, but he never did in China. He gets a lot of oil burns at work. I know he is hurting, but he always tell us it doesn't hurt ... My mom's hands are always in pain because she touches frozen items all the time at work. We always tell her to go see a doctor and one day she finally went. They wanted her to see a specialist but my mom didn't want to go anymore because it would be too expensive. One visit would cost over $1,000 and that is a month and half of her paycheck. Two days ago, she told me to cancel the appointment ... Instead she bought some over-the-counter ointment, which isn't working because her bones are hurting. She is in so much pain that she can't even sleep at 2 o'clock in the morning and then she needs to go to work in the morning again. My mom didn't want to go to work, but she continues to go. My mom works very, very fast, too because she is afraid they would fire her if she slows down.

These are some of the many dilemmas that low-income and working-class immigrant families experience. While a few of the parents were able to find more comfortable working conditions other parents are limited to working in restaurants or factories, which most often do not provide any benefits (Kwong, 1987). Moreover, as Bebe and other youth have shared, many parents often experience downward mobility in their employment as well as hostile and dehumanize treatments.

"Trying to learn English": Adult English classes

In addition to their work schedule, all of the parents either are taking English classes or have done so at one time when they came to the United States. They have all expressed the importance of knowing English; however, while some parents are able to take classes others are not due to their work schedules. Mrs. Mui, for example, took English classes for several years when she arrived in the United States. She expressed how different life in China and the United States are because of the language barrier. She compared the difference in detail:

> In the U.S., the main issue is the language barrier. In China, I am able to handle any challenges that arise. However, in the U.S., things are completely different. For example, the culture is different. I spent a lot of time trying to learn English, but I still don't have a strong handle.

Immigrant parents had to rely and depend on other people for help since coming to the United States due to their minimum English proficiency. As a result, the importance of knowing English is evident for the parents. Mrs. Mui, explained, "It doesn't matter how good of a job is in front of you if you don't know any English. Knowing English increases your chances of getting a good stable job." When I asked the parents what their expectations are for their child(ren), they all stated firmly that they wanted their child(ren) to be healthy, graduate from high school and obtain higher education, find a stable job, and adjust to life in the United States. They do not hope that their children would work in labor-intensive jobs like the ones they currently hold. Mrs. Kam, who has two sons in high school, expressed:

> As parents, we all hope that our children have a better life and are able to adjust to U.S. society because we are unable to do so. We don't know English, which makes it is extremely difficult to fully adjust to the U.S … I don't want my sons to work in menial labor jobs where [they] have to do strenuous labor such as working in restaurants. Everyone knows working in restaurants is extremely hard work. After working 8 to 10 years, you would definitely develop some kind of reoccurring health issues, such as sickness and physical pain. Nobody hopes that their later generations would be doing these kinds of jobs.

Parents are extremely committed to learning English and would attend some form of Adult English program either on their only day off in the week or before or after work. For example, Mr. Mui, who works full-time in an Asian supermarket in Harborview, attends HCCC's Adult English classes for three hours each week on Mondays, his day off. Mr. Mui is enrolled in the one-on-one class rather than the group class because he "hopes to learn English faster." Prior to enrolling in HCCC's Adult English program, he took some English classes at a local church in Chinatown. Similar to Mr. Mui, Mr. and Mrs. Zhang, who are both in their 40s, are enrolled in HCCC's free Adult English classes. Mrs. Zhang works at one of the largest food retailer of natural and organic products and Mr. Zhang is an elder assistant. They came to the United States in mid-2006 with their only child, Jason, who was in 10th grade. They decided to enroll in English class since they "didn't know how to go to places and had no money and job." Mr. and Mrs. Zhang would attend the same morning class and then head to work afterward.

The demand for English classes has increased over the years. As a result, nonprofits and schools have had to turn away applicants. A recent article from a local newspaper reported that the state and local government have been urging businesses with high immigrant employees to offer English classes instead of only relying on nonprofits and schools. A growing number of companies in the state are offering free Adult English classes for their employees. Mrs. Lau is a hotel housekeeper at a hotel. She is currently taking English classes Mondays and Wednesdays that is offered by her labor union. Mrs. Lau noted the importance of being proficient in English, "not knowing any English is a problem to finding jobs in the U.S."

At the same time, a number of parents were unable to take English classes due to work conflicts. Parents who work full-time in ethnic restaurants would usually need to leave their house by 9 or 10 a.m. and not return until 10 or 11 p.m., sometimes even later on the weekends. Parents working in second and third shift jobs are also unable to attend classes since they work from 2 or 3 a.m. to around 12 p.m. noon and then they would need to sleep and do household chores. While they might not have time, parents did take English classes but after a few weeks they had to stop because they realize their time was very limited. A lot of the parents, like Mrs. Lee who works from 2 a.m. to around mid-morning to noon, asserted how they "don't even have the time and energy to read the newspapers."

Similar to other studies (Olsen, 1997, 2000; Tse, 2001), the parents' realities contradict the dominant perception that immigrants do not want to learn English and resist doing so. As I have shown above, parents listed being proficient in English and obtaining an education as highly important for their children and future generations. The parents long inflexible work hours and lack of English were two reasons that affected their contact with their children's schools. At the same time, what happens to immigrant parents when they come into contact with U.S. schools? In the following section, I illustrate the experiences of immigrant parents with the U.S. public school system.

"I don't feel welcome": Immigrant parents and the U.S. school system

> I rarely go to my children's school now. I don't have much contact with their teachers because they don't speak Cantonese or Mandarin. If we went, it would be uncomfortable for everyone because of the language barrier. When my daughter was at a school with a bilingual program, we did attend the parent-teacher conferences ... because some of the school personnel were bilingual and able to communicate with us and explain things. And if there was a non-Chinese speaking teacher, someone at the school was able to help with the translation. The school personnel at that school were good ... Also, now we haven't been able to attend many of their school events because the times always conflicted with our work schedule.
> —MRS. LAU, PARENT

The stories that have filled this chapter have expressed how the triangulated image of tension between parents' levels of knowledge about U.S. schools that are often taken for granted by those who know *and* have access to the system, English ability, and occupation are played out. For example, Mrs. Lau's statement showed how language and time conflicts restricted her from attending many of the school events. However, she also mentions that when the school personnel spoke

Cantonese and were respectful, she was able to find ways to attend meetings with teachers. Interestingly, Mrs. Lau recognizes not only her own discomfort with the language difference, but the discomfort of the teachers as well. Along with the possible collectivist cultural roots of stating that it would be "uncomfortable for everyone," this may also indicate a level of agency generally unrecognized in (low-income) immigrant parents. In spite of this potential sense of agency, the obstacles for the parents remain significant. Parents do want to participate with their children's schools; however, they cannot because they do not speak English due to their rigid work schedules. One parent summed up what many of the parents felt about U.S. schools: "We can't help our children with school anymore."

As I have discussed, "similar to other studies (Adler, 2007; Advocates for Children of New York, 2004; Ji & Koblinsky, 2009; Valdés, 1996), parents routinely felt uncomfortable going to their children's schools due to language and cultural differences" (Wong, 2013, p. 165). Parents expressed numerous times that the language barrier was one of the major reasons for not attending school events. Some of the parents expressed feeling lost and overwhelmed about attending school events. If they did attend, the parents "felt helpless" since they "can't communicate with the teachers." For instance, "I have been to their schools but I never met their teachers because I don't know English," one parent asserted. "It's impossible for me to talk to them." As a result, parents are only limited to saying "hi" to the teachers since they are unable to ask questions. Mrs. Cheung explained how immigrant parents often feel "helpless" and "powerless" as a result of these barriers with the U.S. school system:

> For me the saddest and hardest thing is going to see my children's teachers and not understanding what they are saying. I have a lot of questions that I want to ask the teachers but I am unable to express them. When I say something, they won't understand me. This makes me really helpless.

Jeff, a youth worker, explained how the communication gap between schools and low-income immigrant families has always been an issue, especially during the current high-stakes testing era where immigrant parents are being left behind.

> Achievement is so important. Academic achievement and benchmark is so important that school really failed to reach out to parents, whether it's Cantonese speakers, Spanish speakers, Mandarin or Vietnamese speakers. Schools really, really failed to make that effort. At the same time, schools are limited with resource as well.

Additionally, he noted in detail the structural and institutional policies and practices that create and maintain such barriers between schools and families to initiate the communication.

We have a lot of parents whose schools don't know how to communicate with them. Regardless of benchmarks and academic achievement, you really cannot achieve when you cannot reach out to the parents. You are dealing with a very large immigrant population ... How do you reach out to Chinese parents? Or grandparents? Or Haitian parents? Or Vietnamese? If we cannot communicate with the parents or the guardians, how do you bridge the issues? What I mean is school failed is not because parents don't care; it's just that parents don't know what's going on. Cuz there's so little communication between parents and schools. There are a lot of different reasons. I am not putting all the blame on the school. Schools have so little resources as well. It's just how it's set-up.

As I have mentioned elsewhere (Wong, 2008, 2011, 2013), parents did attend school events during their children's elementary school years because bilingual services and support were available. Attending school events decreases for parents due to the schools' inability to provide appropriate services and welcoming space for many immigrant families, as Mrs. Lau noted at the beginning of this chapter. The lack of multilingual services and cultural awareness and respect is demonstrated by a larger system that perceives difference as a deficit, and thus does not provide language services to those that do not have access to English proficiency. In other words, it is not that parents do not want to attend; rather, due to the unwelcoming environment at many schools immigrant parents eventually stop attending. Similarly, Delgado-Gaitan (2001) found in her research with Latinx[3] parents in California that while the bilingual preschool program was a success in building and maintaining parent relationships, schooling became distant for parents once their children entered elementary school due to the limited resources to assist with the home–school connections. Multicultural school personnel, therefore, serve as a bridge for immigrant parents to feel connected in the space. Furthermore, youth and community workers, such as HCCC, serve as a bridge in opening the doors for immigrant and low-income families.

Additionally, Lew (2006) and Stanton-Salazar's (2001) notions of social class and social capital can be applied here to understand how school systems reflect the larger U.S. society in terms of economic and racial stratification that places and confines low-income and working poor immigrants of color in the margins. While having knowledge about the U.S. school system is crucial, it is not enough if families do not have the same access and opportunities as White middle and upper middle class families. In order to develop and maintain culturally responsive home–school relations with immigrant and low-income communities, we first must examine the complexity of the families' situations. Through his continuous work with immigrant families, Jeff, who has worked at CYC and in the community for ten plus years, made the following observation:

The community is parents who are poor, that's a fact. Parents who are poor really have to work to feed and clothe their children, and put a roof over their heads. I mean that's the reality ... They can't afford to leave work because they can't miss an extra $50 in a day. So there are different factors and justifications ... I mean that's really what it is—immigrant parents basically live paycheck to paycheck. So to assume that they are not trying or don't care, is not real. It's fiction.

Jeff explained how the work situations for low-income and working-class immigrants are extremely complex, especially poor and low-income communities. Particularly, living in a "capitalist system" like the United States where being low-income and working-class *and* an immigrant of color are factors that confine parents. The issues faced by parents are similar to those faced by all working poor and working-class parents (e.g., Lareau, 2000).

Another obstacle for families' limited interactions with teachers and school is the hours for parent–teacher conferences, which usually occur in the mornings to early afternoons, and open houses are between 5 p.m. and 8 p.m. And since the majority of the parents work second shift jobs, they are at work or have just got out of work during those times and thus are unable to attend such events. For parents who work in restaurants and other non-nine to five jobs, attending school events becomes a challenge. Amanda, a second year college student, who started coming to CYC in 5th grade shortly after she immigrated to the United States, said she did not tell her mother about the parent–teacher conferences and open houses because of the time conflict with her mother's waitressing job at a Chinese restaurant:

She didn't attend them [school events]. I didn't tell her about them because I know she won't have time. A lot of the open houses are 7–8 o'clock at night. She works up until 10 o'clock at night. There's no way in restaurant and cook society, there's no such thing as taking off.

Similarly, Nicole, a second generation Chinese American and a 9th grader, shared her parents' challenges with the U.S. educational system: "they don't understand and can't communicate with the teachers." As a result, young people are aware of their parents' demanding work schedules and language barrier and thus often do not inform them about school events.

Schools with bilingual teachers and staffs

Successful bilingual and bicultural schools are able to create and maintain communication with parents and the community. For instance, I (Wong, 2008) noted how some of the youth expressed the importance of schools having cultural connections of their students and the surrounding community. Half of the youth in this research attended Hope Elementary School and they remembered the various events at school. In acknowledging their diverse student population, Hope Elementary School hosts cultural events throughout the school year, such as the Lunar New Year celebration where students would perform various Chinese dances and musical instruments. Unlike the families in Valdés's research (1996) and some of the youth in this research who attended other bilingual schools, the report cards, memos, and announcements from the school were in both Chinese and English. Parents were able to use the bilingual materials to go from not knowing the system to knowing it and advocating for their children.

Parents attended their children's school events when they were in bilingual programs because they can communicate with the teachers. However, many did not attend once their child entered all English speaking classrooms due to the language differences. According to Betty, her parents attended "school conferences and open houses when I was in elementary school, because the teachers spoke Cantonese. Now, in middle school, my parents don't go because they can't communicate with my teachers." In other words, the teachers in the bilingual school were more accessible because they were able to communicate with her parents and parents are able to express themselves much easier. Some of the parents were able to seek help from teachers who were bilingual, even after their child(ren) have graduated from the class. Essentially, the following quotes are examples of how low-income immigrant parents learned to navigate the U.S. educational system through the assistance and resource of their children's bilingual and bicultural teachers. When Jerry was admitted to an elite public high school, Mrs. Ho was able to obtain advice from his elementary school teacher:

> I went to Jerry's fifth grade teacher. He was a good teacher. I asked the teacher if he was free and if I could ask him some questions. He told me he was and so I told him that Jerry was admitted to [this school] and I don't know if I should let him go. I told him that I asked around and they all told me those students are bad. He told me, "since your son was admitted to that school, I suggest letting him go. All of the students who got admitted must have decent grades in order to make it in. Additionally, this school is ranked one of the top 5 public high schools in Harborview and so the teachers and students should be better." He told me since Jerry made it in, I should let him try it out.

Mrs. Kam reflected on her experiences with her son's fifth grade teacher:

> When Vincent was in middle school, he had a teacher from Hong Kong who was really good. If there were anything, the teacher would call me. The teacher also gave me the classroom phone number and told me to feel free to call if I needed anything.

In other words, the parents found having bilingual and bicultural teachers more accessible if they have questions about school-related matters. They felt comfortable in going in or calling the teachers for advices. Moreover, these two examples show how parents learned to navigate the school system through the assistance of bilingual and bicultural teachers.

I have thus far illustrated the complexity that low-income and working poor immigrant parents experience daily. Specifically, the triangulated tension of their limited English ability, level of knowledge about U.S. schools, and work are all intertwined inextricably for them. Therefore, my work reconfirms the work of earlier studies as discussed in Chapter 1. At the same time, examination and understanding must lead to well-conceived actions. In Chapter 5, I will show how the parents found a supportive network and learned to navigate and negotiate the U.S. school system through HCCC.

Notes

1. Throughout this book, I use the terms "Community Worker" and "Youth Worker" interchangeably.
2. As activist scholars, the power of terminologies is important, and thus needs to be acknowledged in all research. For instance, I use "parents" because all of the youths were from one or two parent households. At the same time, we must be aware and inclusive of the diverse forms of family structures (e.g., single parent, caregiver(s), LGBTQIA+, adoption, etc.).
3. Latinx is the gender-neutral term for Latino, Latina, and Latin@ as it acknowledges people who are LGBTIA+ and gender nonconforming.

Works cited

Adler, S. M. (2007). Hmong home-school relations: Hmong parents and professionals speak out. In C. C. Park, R. Endo, S. J. Lee, & X. L. Rong (Eds.), *Asian American education: Acculturation, literacy development, and learning* (pp. 77–104). Charlotte, NC: Information Age Publishing.

Advocates for Children. (2004). *Denied at the door: Language barriers block immigrant parents from school involvement.* New York, NY: Advocates for Children.

Bourdieu, P. (1986). The forms of capital. In J. Richardson (Ed.), *Handbook of theory and research for the sociology of education* (pp. 241–258). New York: Greenwood Press.

Collingnon, F. F., Men, M., & Tan S. (2001). Finding ways in: Community-based perspectives on Southeast Asian family involvement in a New England state. *Journal of Education for Students Placed at Risk, 6*(1 and 2), 27–44.

Delgado-Gaitan, C. (2001). *The power of community: Mobilizing for family and schooling.* Lanham, MD: Rowman & Littlefield.

Delgado-Gaitan, C. (2004). *Involving Latino families in schools: Raising student achievement through home-school partnerships.* Thousand Oaks, CA: Corwin Press.

González, N. E., Moll, L., & Amanti, C. (2005). *Funds of knowledge: Theorizing practices in households, communities and classrooms.* Mahwah, NJ: Lawrence Erlbaum Associates.

González, N., Moll, L., Tenery, M. F., Rivera, A., Rendon, P., Gonzales, R., & Amanti, C. (1995). Funds of knowledge for teaching in Latino households. *Urban Education, 29*(4), 444–471.

Hune, S., & Takeuchi, D. (2008). *Asian Americans in Washington State: Closing Their Hidden Achievement Gaps.* A report submitted to The Washington State Commission on Asian Pacific American Affairs. Seattle, WA: University of Washington.

Ji, C. S., & Koblinsky, S. A. (2009). Parent involvement in children's education: An exploratory study of urban, Chinese immigrant families. *Urban Education, 44*(6), 687–709.

Kibria, N. (1993). *Family tightrope: The changing lives of Vietnamese Americans.* Princeton, NJ: Princeton University Press.

Kwong, P. (1987). *The new Chinatown.* New York, NY: Hill and Wang.

Lareau, A. (2000). *Home advantage: Social class and parental intervention in elementary education.* Lanham, MD: Rowman & Littlefield Publishers.

Lee, S. J., & Kumashiro, K. K. (2005). *A report on the status of Asian Americans and Pacific Islanders in education: Beyond the "model minority" stereotype.* Washington, DC: National Education Association.

Lew, J. (2006). *Asian Americans in class: Charting the achievement gap among Korean American youth.* New York, NY: Teachers College Press.

Li, G. (2010). Social class, culture, and "good parenting": Voices of low-SES families. In M. M. March & T. Turner-Vorbeck (Eds.), *(Mis)Understanding families: Learning from real families in our schools* (pp. 162–178). New York, NY: Teachers College Press.

Olsen, L. (1997). *Made in America: Immigrant students in our public schools.* New York, NY: New Press.

Olsen, L. (2000). Learning English and learning America: Immigrants in the center of a storm. *Theory into Practice, 39*(4), 196–202.

Ong, A. (2003). *Buddha is hiding: Refugees, citizenship, the new America.* Berkeley, CA: University of California Press.

Phelan, P., Davidson, A. L., & Yu, H. C. (1998). *Adolescents' worlds: Negotiating family, peers, and school.* New York, NY: Teachers College Press.

Portes, A., & Rumbaut, R. G. (2001). *Legacies: The story of the immigrant second generation.* Berkeley, CA: University of California Press.

Qin, D. B. (2006). "Our child doesn't talk to us anymore": Alienation in immigrant Chinese families. *Anthropology & Educational Quarterly, 37*(2), 162–179.

Sakamoto, A., & Xie, Y. (2006). The socioeconomic attainments of Asian Americans. In P. G. Min (Ed.), *Asian Americans: Contemporary trends and issues* (2nd ed., pp. 54–77). Thousand Oaks, CA: Pine Forge Press.

Siu, S. F. (2002). Toward building home-school partnerships: The case of Chinese American families and public schools. In E. H. Tamura, V. Chattergy, & R. Endo (Eds.), *Asian and*

Pacific Islander American education: Social, cultural, and historical contexts (pp. 59–84). South El Monte, CA: Pacific Asia Press.

Stanton-Salazar, R. D. (2001). *Manufacturing hope and despair: The school and kin support networks of U.S.-Mexican youth.* New York, NY: Teachers College Press.

Suárez-Orozco, C., & Suárez-Orozco, M. M. (2001). *Children of immigration.* Cambridge, MA: Harvard University Press.

Tse, L. (2001). *"Why don't they learn English?": Separating fact from fallacy in the U.S. language debate.* New York, NY: Teachers College Press.

Valdés, G. (1996). *Con respecto: Bridging the distances between culturally diverse families and schools.* New York, NY: Teachers College Press.

What Kids Can Do. (2006). *Forty-cent tip: Stories of New York City immigrant workers.* By the Students of Three New York Public International High Schools. Providence, RI: Next Generation Press.

Wong, N. W. A. (2008). "They see us as resource": The role of a community-based youth center in supporting the academic lives of low-income Chinese American youth. *Anthropology & Education Quarterly, 39*(2), 181–204.

Wong, N. W. A. (2010). "Cuz they care about the people who goes there": The multiple roles of a community-based youth center in providing "Youth (Comm)Unity" for low-income Chinese American youth. *Urban Education, 45*(5), 708–739.

Wong, N. W. A. (2011). Broadening support for AAPI immigrant families: The role and impact of community-based organizations in family-community-school partnerships. *AAPI Nexus Journal: Policy, Practice, and Community, Special Issue: White House Initiative on Asian Americans and Pacific Islanders, 9*(1 and 2), 134–142.

Wong, N. W. A. (2013). "Like a bridge": How a community-based organization helps immigrant and working poor Chinese parents navigate U.S. schools. In R. Endo & X. L. Rong (Eds.), *Educating Asian Americans: Achievement, schooling, and identities* (pp. 181–204). Charlotte, NC: Information Age Publishing.

CHAPTER FOUR

Youths' relationship with family and school

Becky, a 1.5 generation and an eighth grader in 2007, immigrated to the United States two years prior at the age of eleven with her parents. I recall a thirteen-year-old Becky describing "life was simpler in China." For instance, a typical weekday started with her parents going to work and Becky going to school. In the evenings, her mom would prepare a scrumptious dinner and the family would always eat together. During the weekends and holidays, family time was a whole day's event. However, "our lives changed after immigrating to the U.S." Due to language barriers, her parents' only opportunity was to work long and tiresome hours in ethnic restaurants. Family time was limited and as a result, she was alone the majority of the time while her parents were away at work. Becky reflects on the hardships because of the exhausting work hours and intensive labor her parents endure daily: "It was difficult since my mom and dad work in the restaurants. I would see them very briefly in the morning and then sometimes late at night." Moreover, at the age of eleven, she quickly realized the need to mature and be the connector for her family with dominant U.S. culture. When we reconnected in 2015, she recently graduated from a local private four-year university. Becky mentioned the similarities that she and the other youth at CYC have. For instance, having immigrant parents who do not know English, and thus forced to work in ethnic restaurants. Today, Becky continues to serve as a bridge for her immigrant parents with the dominant society. She explains:

I learned that all of the youth at CYC share very similar backgrounds. Like many parents, my mom and dad work in ethnic restaurants, because they don't know any English. As a result, growing up, I served as a bridge for my parents with the outside world. I am their translator and connector. Today, my parents still work in the restaurant industry. However, since I graduated from college, I am glad that they don't need to work as hard.

Becky's experience reveals that youth of color from low-income immigrant families often struggle with language and cultural adjustment, poverty, hostility, and racism in the United States (see, e.g., Lee, 1996, 2001, 2005; Li, 2002; Lopez, 2003; Olsen, 1997; Suárez-Orozco & Suárez-Orozco, 2001; Valdés, 1996, 2001; Valenzuela, 1999). Additionally, scholars (Lee, 2001, 2005; Valenzuela, 1999) have noted that students of color routinely perceive a lack of "authentic caring" in the schools to the point of experiencing schools as a space of "subtractive schooling" and not feeling comfortable in schools (Lee, 2005; Lopez, 2003; Olsen, 1997; Roffman, Suárez-Orozco, & Rhodes, 2003; Valenzuela, 1999; Wong, 2008). The young people in these studies often have expressed that their teachers and administrators have "fail[ed] to forge meaningful connections with their students," which could lead to withdrawal from school (Valenzuela, 1999, p. 5). The youth in my research also share similar views; and thus, they were most comfortable beyond the school settings. Essentially, many youth repeatedly expressed "CYC became my second home and family." This chapter illuminates the youths' relationship with their family and schools. I will first discuss the impact long and tiresome workdays have on parent–child relationships. Then I will amplify the young people's experiences in and with U.S. schools.

Always at work: The impact of long workdays on parent–child relationships

Children of immigrants from low-income and working-class backgrounds—like those in this research—often are left unsupervised because their parents work long hours in low-paying jobs that do not offer much of a flexible schedule (Lew, 2004; Li, 2003; Lopez, 2003; Louie, 2004; Min, 1998; Suárez-Orozco & Suárez-Orozco, 2001). In her research of a Chinese Canadian immigrant family, Li (2003) explains, the parents' long work hours "prevented them from spending time with their children" and thus children were left on their own during the after school hours and on the weekends (p. 189). As a result, children of immigrants from low-income and working-class households are frequently apart from their parents before and after school hours and on weekends. Moreover,

due to their limited English skills, many of the parents are unable to participate and negotiate in their children's academics as well as social and emotional
well-being (Phelan, Davidson, & Yu, 1993; Roffman et al., 2003; Suárez-Orozco
& Suárez-Orozco, 2001). Therefore, the youth oftentimes are left to handle
and figure out matters on their own—forcing them to take on adult roles at
a much earlier age than their upper middle class peers. In other words, these
youth become "hyper-responsible" children at a very early age (Suárez-Orozco
& Suárez-Orozco, 2001; Wong, 2010). The CYC staff members have shared
experiences through their interactions with the youth and families. Cindy, the
Tutor Coordinator at CYC, captured the realities of the many families that CYC
serves—parents have limited interactions with their children because of their
long and inflexible work hours.

> [B]ased on my experience talking to the teens, they really do have limited time in
> speaking with their parents and also because ... a lot of the parents work really late ...
> they would see their parents like within a week, 4–5 times ... or even talk to them. So
> it's really lack of time, busy schedules for the parents. So I would say that a lot of our
> teens do not communicate that well with their parents.

Calvin, a 1.5 generation and a sixth grader, explained when his parents come home
late from work he is left to take care of himself. Because of his parents' work schedule being so compacted, Calvin rarely sees them. Calvin's father works six days a
week for more than ten hours each day as a construction worker. Calvin's mother
works at a Japanese restaurant that is about an hour's drive from Harborview and
returns home past 11 p.m. Therefore, during the nonschool hours, Calvin cares for
himself. "I wish we could sometimes eat dinner together," expressed Calvin.

A number of young people currently live or have lived with one parent or
other relatives due to their parents' long work hours. I met sixteen-year-old Maggie, who immigrated to the United States in 2005 with her father and thirteen-
year-old younger sister. During high school, Maggie and her sister lived with their
two aunts and cousins because their father worked in another state. Her father
returns to Harborview every few months, and thus the aunts handle all of their
school and daily matters. However, while she understands the sacrifice, Maggie
misses her father immensely. She also has added responsible—having to care for
her younger sister and herself since their parents are divorced.

The parents' work has a huge affect on children of immigrants, particularly
since the youth end up with greater responsibilities and they are separated from
their parents for most of the day, which often result in communication barriers.
One of the CYC staff elaborated on the parent–child relationships of the many
youth who come to CYC:

A lot of the parents are quite busy due to work responsibilities; and so to even sit down to have dinner or go out together as a family is rare, which leads to low parent-children communications and interactions. As a result, relationships become distant and conflicts and misunderstanding often occur. When the parent(s) are free, they would tell their children to do this or take this, but they rarely go on vacation or around the city. I truly believe with some of the recent immigrant youth, they might have adults in their lives but they might not have adults who can "connect" with them, especially if their parents work long hours.

When families have networks and resources present in the United States, they are able to utilize them for assistance (e.g., childcare, jobs, and housing). For example, Bobby, a U.S. born youth and an eighth grader, lived with his aunt, grandparents, and cousins in a neighborhood of Harborview for seven years while his parents lived in Chinatown. He explained, "My parents need to work. They work in the restaurants and so my parents didn't have time to take care of me. That's why I lived with my aunt." On the other hand, if families do not have the support and resources available to them in the United States, their only option is to ask family members in China. Some of the U.S. born youth, for instance, were sent to live with their grandparents in China when they were a few months old. They were raised by their grandparents for three to four years and then came back to the United States once they were old enough to register for school. Philip, a graduating high school senior, was brought to China when he was 6 months old where his maternal grandparents and family cared for him. Philip lived in China for more than two years and "before I turned three, I came back to Harborview." Philip's mother, Ms. Chan, explained about being a recent immigrant and not having any support and resource in the United States: "at the time, sending Philip to live with my parents in China was the only option for me."

Tommy, a graduating high school senior, was sent to live with his maternal grandmother in China while his older brother and parents remained in the United States. His parents worked in Chinese restaurants. Tommy's mother is a waitress while his father, now retired, was a chef for nearly thirty years. With their long and labor-intensive work schedule, Tommy explains, "My parents were not able to take care of my older brother and me." As a result, their paternal grandmother, who lives in Harborview's Chinatown, cared for his older brother. Then when Tommy was born, his paternal grandmother "couldn't watch two small kids and so I was brought to China when I was a month old." At the age of four, Tommy returned to Harborview where he lived with his paternal grandmother and older brother in Chinatown because of his parents' long work hours in restaurants. He noted, "My parents worked a lot. They were always working when I was growing up." However, no matter how busy, Tommy and his family would always have family dinner every Tuesdays, because that was the only day his parents along with many families who worked in ethnic restaurants have off.

Similar to the other young people in this research, Tommy became "very independent" at an early age. He recalled "taking the subway when I was 10 years old with my friends and neighbors." We would look at the subway map and say "Oh, let's go there. So I wasn't too 'dependent' on my family." Moreover, since his parents worked long hours in restaurants, Tommy was alone a lot and thus "I kept a lot of things to myself." As a result, Tommy's living situations have—from being sent to China to be taken care of to living with his paternal grandmother in Chinatown—impacted his relationship with his parents. While Tommy has grown to understand and appreciate his parents (which he accredited CYC for assisting), the process is nevertheless ongoing. More importantly, the young people's experiences illustrate the urgent need to create and maintain a strong and continual support system for them. In addition to parents and other family members who are unable to provide them with the kind of support and assistance that they seek, the young people expressed having "uncaring" teachers and administrators, which I will turn to now.

"They don't even care": Relationships with schools and school personnel

The youth voiced numerous times how teachers "don't even care" about the students. For instance, Wendy, a graduating high school senior who was born and raised in Harborview, was asked if teachers cared about students. She provided the following response:

Wendy:	Some [laughs]. Cuz I remember some during middle school they're really caring; but now when I think of my high school, some of them just don't care.
Anjela:	What do you mean?
Wendy:	Cuz I remember a few teachers, when the bell ring, "Kids, drop the books," grab her bag and said, "See ya class" and ran out the door.
Anjela:	So she ran out the door?
Wendy:	Yeah. And then the class was like still picking up their stuff. I was like, "Okay."
Anjela:	Maybe she had to go somewhere that day?
Wendy:	She did this everyday, like you can't have that much of a busy schedule. That's impossible.
Anjela:	What kind of teachers do you see at school then?

Wendy: Teachers who come to school, they teach and than they take breaks and they teach again and they go home. I mean, yeah. Like there are a few teachers, they are like, "Oh, if you needed extra help or something," they'll probably be like, "Oh, stay after school today and I'll help you." Like some teachers they say that but then when after school comes, they're not there like they just flowed out the door. But some teachers, when they say it they're actually there.

While Wendy noted some of her teachers were caring, what she remembered the most was teachers who did not care.

Sarah, who was an eighth grader in 2005, expressed similar testimonies. She said, "School is boring. I learn nothing there, only learn how to sleep more." Sarah also voiced, "The teachers don't even care about us. When we're out of their classes, they're like 'Oh, go ahead.' They don't even care if we jump off the building. That's how I feel … the teachers just don't care." When I asked her to elaborate, Sarah responded, "Because after the last bell rings you are out of their responsibilities." Two years later in 2007, when I asked Sarah, who was now a sophomore in high school, if her teachers and counselor were caring, she responded with the following:

It depends on the teacher, like if the teacher is really nice and friendly you actually feel like you could talk about anything to that teacher; but if the teacher is really strict and like distant and always degrades you then you don't feel like you want to talk with them. They don't care. Like they'll say, "You can't make it to college. You're stupid. Don't even think about it." My teacher said that to my whole class. We always get the lowest grades and so she just said those things to us. She always burst these things out. Everyday she tells us "you guys are the worse class I have ever taught in all my years of teaching."

The youth mentioned some of their teachers at schools lacked "commitment." For instance, Calvin reflected on his high school volleyball experience where he coached and managed the team:

Most of the teachers, especially in the public schools, could learn an element or skill about commitment to their students. For example, my volleyball coach, who was also a calculus teacher at the school. I was hoping to talk to him about volleyball and anything, but there was no commitment at all. I hope he won't hear this. There's no commitment. I have to coach the team. I have to manage the team. It was just a lot of work. I couldn't really talk to him because he is always running errands. It's just commitment. It's just being there for the youth or even your own students.

Amy reflects on her K-12 schooling and explains a lack of commitment and care from her teachers:

In the day to day classrooms, no one wants to be there, except for an exception few. And the teachers just go about themselves until class start. I am sure there are better teachers out there, I just never had that.

Sarah also shared discouragements and lack of support and commitment from her high school guidance counselor:

My guidance counselor told my friend that he couldn't go to college cuz his grades were too low. That's how wonderful my guidance counselor is. She told him he should get his GED. He was a senior. He got into a public university; but she told him that he can't go to any college, cuz his grades are too low.

Furthermore, many of the youth do not know the name of their guidance counselors. On the same subject, Steven remarked, "I don't even know how to find the guidance counselors." Cindy, CYC's Tutoring Coordinator, expressed similar sentiments based on her work with the youth:

[The] majority of the youth don't even have the time to talk with their teachers. You'd only get like 10–15 minutes to talk to a teacher. If you ask some of the youth, they don't even know their guidance [counselor]. "Who's that? Never heard of that."

The young people generally do not have a close relationship with their teachers and rarely have contact with their guidance counselors at school; and thus these gatekeepers (Carter, 2005; Conchas, 2006) are invisible and inaccessible in the maze of the school system.

Bobby, a ninth grader, defines a "good teacher" as being "able to explain something to you until you get it and in a nice way, too. They have to care for their students." Similarly, Alan indicated that a "good" teacher is someone who "cares" about their students and "makes class more fun." Alan described an "ideal teacher" as "someone who [is] just like any other person and when outside of school they actually say hi. And they don't judge you and would communicate and like help you on problems." Similarly, Johnny commented, "School is supposed to be a fun learning place, instead of a prison. It's like you have to do work all the time and they don't care, no fun." In other words, the youth "are committed to an *authentic* form of caring that emphasizes relations of reciprocity between teachers and students" (Valenzuela, 1999, p. 61). The youth expressed feeling alienated from many of their teachers and guidance counselors. As noted in Rosenbloom and Way (2004), "students felt that a caring teacher should help students when they did not understand the material, control the students in the classroom, and maintain high expectations by encouraging students to study and achieve academically" (p. 436). I should note that with the dismantling of our public schools, increasing class sizes, and demand of high-stakes standardization in school districts across the United States, particularly in urban settings, such relationships become even more difficult.

The young people in this research often expressed the invisibility of Asian and Asian American experiences in their school curriculum. The young people are searching for a culturally relevant education (Ladson-Billings, 1995a). They have strongly remarked that schools should include the experiences of Asian Pacific Islander Americans in their curriculum where they could empower themselves and educate their community. Some of the young people associated caring to teachers knowing and teaching about Asian American experiences. Brian, a graduating high school senior, reflected on his K-12 schooling experience, "I wish they would stop teaching U.S. history so much. You take that during elementary school and then in middle school, you take U.S. history *again*. And then in high school, you take U.S. history *again*." When I asked him to elaborate, Brian added:

> Well, I never learn about Asian Americans. I didn't learn about anything other than just like America under the 13 colonies. They started back there and then slowly talking about Jamestown, Mayflower and everything. They never got into like any other race ... So U.S. history is representing White people, like I don't see anything else in it. It's all just wars and America winning battles and everything. For example, they only got as far as to say the Japanese bombed Pearl Harbor. That's it. Like that's the only words I saw. They never even mentioned Japanese Americans being in internment camps. They just said the Japanese bombed America. And I'm like, that's it. And they just went on to the next chapter.

Other youth, such as Allyson, a high school freshman, likewise noted, "Schools don't talk about Asians in the U.S. They never taught us anything about Asians being in the U.S." Ling, a sophomore in high school, explained the importance of learning about Asian American experiences and issues and how schools never incorporated the experiences:

> Through CYC, I got to meet Helen Zia at the conference and you showed us the documentary on Vincent Chin and you did the Angel Island workshop ... I learned more about Asians in America from these experiences, cuz I didn't know much about that. Schools should teach us more because it is important to see ourselves, not only White people's history, in the curriculum. Most of the time we learn about White people's history. Asians are included but most of the times they are included during wars like when the U.S. fought with Japan and when one of the presidents went to visit China. That's it.

As a result, the experiences of "the Other" are silenced in many of our schools nationwide. The youth understand the hidden curriculum in their schools. Similar statements were echoed from other young people as they reflected on the school curriculum. In other words, Valenzuela (1999) writes "the most important step is to introduce a culture of authentic caring that incorporates all members of the school community as valued and respected partners in education" (p. 99). As I have illustrated earlier, the youth do not always feel comfortable in their schools because of what appears to be the lack of a culturally relevant education and understanding (Ladson-Billings, 1995a) and the absence of authentic caring from schools (Valenzuela, 1999).

In the following section, I will share the youths' experiences and interactions with U.S. public schools. Particularly, I will amplify the young people's testimonies of the daily exclusions, racial discriminations, tensions, and invisibility in multiracial and multiethnic urban middle and high schools. These testimonies from the young people illuminate another form of disempowerment and disadvantage that low-income and working-class immigrant families struggle with in the United States. At the same time, it is important to point out that these are their testimonies. I did not observe their schools or interview school personnel; nor is my intent to compare the youths' school world with their out-of-school-time world, rather the purpose is to amplify their experiences in U.S. schools as Asians and Asian American youth.

"We are invisible": Asian American youth in U.S. schools

> *I am an Asian*
> *who people*
> *don't see.*
>
> *I am a person*
> *who people*
> *ignore.*
> *I am an Asian?*
> *I am a person?*
> *I am an Asian person* ... (cited in Wing, 1971–1974)

The young people expressed in great depth the impact of institutional and systemic racism and the negative affects of exclusion, racial discriminations, tensions, and stereotypes in U.S. schools; and thus, the poem above is an example of how Asian American youth continue to grapple with their identities and the lack of visibility in dominant U.S. culture. For instance, many of the youth described their struggles with the model minority stereotype in their schools, where they are pressured and expected to meet the stereotype. A second generation and a ninth grader, Allyson noted, "people at school always curse out on Asians, like 'Oh you're Asian, you're suppose to be smart and all these things.'" Allyson also shared the danger of students and teachers (un)consciously interpreting and acting upon stereotypes and their biases in school and classrooms.

> People at [my school] would always come to me with questions because they say 'oh, you're Asian'. Because I'm Asian, then I have to be smart. Then teachers would pick on me. The teachers often say, 'you guys need to start acting like the Asian students in this class. For example, Allyson and [the other Asian student].' Everyone's reply was like 'they're Asian. They're smart.'

Another ninth grader echoed similar experiences:

> In school, Asians are known as smart, not strong; so the dorky, smart and weak Asian. People in class, like teachers and students, would look at me for answers all the time. I feel pressured, cuz other people expect you to be smart in math and science.

While the model minority stereotype labels Asian Americans as highly successful and the "whiz kids" (Brand, 1987) the "perpetual foreigner" stereotype portrays Asian Americans as inherently foreign and therefore "un-American." In her study about Hmong American high school students, Lee (2005) argues, "the school's culture privileges White, middle class students, and marks Hmong American students as racialized outsiders" (p. 47). Anna, a seventh grader and a 1.5 generation, explained candidly how Asians and Chinese Americans are "not really American":

> You can be Asian American, but you're not really American; cuz you're Asian, you look different. If you're born here you'll be Chinese American. This place is call America. And you're not White, so you're not American.

As a result, Anna and the other youth equate U.S. Americans with Whites. As other scholars have argued, we need to "critical[ly] unmask" (Chang & Au, 2007/2008) and challenge the racist stereotypes and oppressions that harm Asian Americans and other communities of color.

With the exception of less than a handful of schools that the youth attended in the Harborview school district, Black and Latinx students are the largest student population. For instance, Cityview High School, a traditional pubic high school, is known for its basketball team, which has won several state championships within the past ten years. At the time of this research, the school served over 1,100 students: African Americans (45.6%), Latinx (26.5%), Asian American (20.8%), White (6.4%), and American Indian (0.7%) students. Cityview High School is the only high school in the district with language-specific Shelter English Immersion

(SEI) high school programs. The students are divided into smaller learning academies ("houses"). One of the academies is the SEI track. The CYC youth who attend Cityview are all recent immigrants from Hong Kong or southern China and in the SEI track.

According to the youth, the most prominent racial and ethnic populations at Cityview were Blacks and Asians, respectively, and "there are only a few Whites." The youth did not differentiate between African American and Latinx students, because, as several youth expressed, "they have similar skin tones." In other words, they equated African Americans and Latinx with sameness, and thus comments such as "it's hard to know how to tell Blacks and Latinos apart" were common. As recent immigrants, these youth have learned (1) the U.S. racial discourse is limited to a binary perspective and (2) such binary is fixated on a Black and White discourse. The danger, however, is that the dominant U.S. racial discourse denies and silences the experiences of communities that do not "fit" the racial binary (e.g., Asians and Pacific Islanders, Indigenous Peoples, Latinx, and multiracial and ethnic individuals) (Ancheta, 1998; Cho, 1993; Kim, 2003; Lee, 2005). If mentioned or discussed, "non-African people of color are categorized as either Black or white" (Cho, 1993, p. 206). Therefore, the youth are aware of the racial hierarchy where Whites and Whiteness are placed at the center of control and power while Blacks and Blackness are at the margins. At the same time, as recent immigrants, they are still constructing the U.S. racialization process. As a result, comments like "I can't tell ..." were expressed. Moreover, due to their tracked classes such understanding is even harder for the Chinese immigrant students since they rarely interact with students from the other academies (Rosenbloom & Way, 2004). Public schools across the United States have shifted from the Black and White student demographics. Instead, schools are racially, ethnically, linguistically, and generationally diverse settings. In 2014, Students of Color became the "new majority" in U.S. public schools (Hussar & Bailey, 2014). Nonetheless, "race-talks" are often silenced, muted, and ignored in schools, which results in "legitimizing Whiteness" (Castagno, 2008) and results in "colormute" (Pollock, 2004).

Several of the youth noted experiencing racial discrimination and stereotypical actions made by some of their non-SEI track peers. Also, while Cityview has a diverse student population, racial tensions exist between the recent Chinese immigrant students in the SEI track and the non-SEI student population, who are predominately Black and Latinx. Bebe, a tenth grader at the school, asserted how the non-SEI students "constantly use the F word and they would say how Chinese is this and that. They would say things like 'I will never go to a Chinese restaurant anymore'." Ka-Kay, also a tenth grader at the school, shared an incident when one of her friends was "bullied" by a Black student:

My friend's locker was next to a Black student. The girl told my friend to move and find another locker, because she didn't want my friend's locker to be next to hers. My friend didn't move because it was her locker. All of a sudden the girl punched my friend right in the eye. My friend felt really dizzy and had a black eye afterwards. These things happen to us on a daily basis.

Education, as one of several institutions that maintain systems of oppression and privilege (Ore, 2003), is central to maintaining systems of oppression and privilege based on race, class, gender, and sexuality. Thus, when school personnel do not address the issues, they are pitting students against one another, and thus create and maintain tension, misunderstandings, and reinforce the dominant oppressive structures. In other words, such actions are forms of White supremacy in maintaining the current U.S. social order.

The "silencing" in critical analysis and reflection of race, privilege, and oppression creates hostile school environments for many of the young people and their peers. Another reason for the continuous discriminations and tensions is due to the tracking of students into different academic areas (Oakes, 1985; Olsen, 1997; Rosenbloom & Way, 2004). As a result, students at Cityview are isolated from their peers in other academies. For example, because they do not take any classes together, the recent Chinese immigrant students in the SEI track do not have any interactions with the non-SEI students, the majority are not recent Chinese immigrants. When I asked the young people how many floors were at the school, none of them knew. Ka-Kay and Bebe, for instance, both guessed six floors but they were not exactly certain because the SEI track students "don't go up and use the other floors," noted Ka-Kay, "because we don't have class there." While the school has five levels, the SEI track students use only two of the floors.

Even though SEI students can transfer out to other academies after they completed the SEI sequence, most remain there. Yee-Mun explained, "I don't like the idea of taking general education classes because some of the students are really 'rude' to us." Similar to Olsen (1997) and Lee (2005), I would argue that the SEI track offers the recent Chinese immigrant students a safe and accepting space. As a result, the only times all students interact with one another were during free periods, change of classes, and before and after school. In other words, they are physically removed and divided in the school for the majority of the school day, which causes and heightens misunderstandings and tensions. Similarly, Suárez-Orozco, Suárez-Orozco, and Todorova (2008) explained the dangers when schools divide students into different houses/academies that provides minimal interactions: "this barrier was hard to break through because the programs are divided physically as well as socially. Typically students in these programs did not share classes, and there were no structures provided by the schools for healthy interactions" (p. 144). Since students are separated into different academies, the only contact they have with each other is through passing in the hallways. During such times, Chinese immigrant students feel the least safe. Yee-Mun, also a tenth grader at the school, recollected:

> Some of the non-SEI students don't like it when we go to their floors. They would throw stuff at us like pens, papers, candies, and coins when we go down or up the stairs … As a result, the Chinese SEI students would usually stay with each other in case something ever happens to one of us. However, one time it was pretty bad. Someone threw a text-book like those thick biology textbooks at a girl's head. The girl couldn't take it any more so she told one of our SEI teachers. Our teacher was really angry by the incident and so for a few weeks she walked with us to our classes on the other floor. She also spoke to the principal and then the school opened a stairway, which was intended for emergency pur-poses like fire drills and such. Only the SEI students were allowed to use that staircase. A security guard was on each floor, too. They would watch us when we change classes. Even to this day, the security guard is still securing the place. They also talked to each of the academic area's coordinator. Since that day, there hasn't been any more throwing.

Besides changing classes, racial tensions occur during other portions of the school day. For instance, Bebe shared several episodes:

> There are a lot of recent immigrant and Black students at the school. The Black students are not that nice. They bully us. They don't really "respect" us because they would scare us. One time a friend of mine was heading to the bathroom and there were no adults in the hallway so a group of Black girls surrounded her. They asked her for money, but she didn't have any that day. So when people hear these things, they think our school is horrible and dangerous. I've experienced similar things as well. This wasn't too long ago, about 2 to 3 weeks ago. A "Black person" walked passed me, and he screamed right in my face and then started laughing frantically. He was laugh-ing so hard, like he was really enjoying it. I gave him a look. I thought he was really immature. Then last summer, I attended summer school to prepare for the state man-dated exam, because I just came to the U.S. a few months earlier. One of the students put their arm on my shoulder and I shook it off, but the student kept putting their arm back on my shoulder and I kept shaking it off. Then the student said, "I got AIDS, you got AIDS now." Everyone in the class started laughing. I immediately left the room.

Other young people have also experienced similar acts of racisms and exclusions. Tommy, a graduating high school senior, recalled one of his visits to his older brother's high school, located in a city right outside of Harborview:

> My brother didn't really like the school because the discrimination and racism was really serious there. The White students always start trouble. They would always tor-ment and start fights with the Asian students. One time when I went to use the bathroom, a group of White students surrounded me. It was a really scary scene. I was 14 years old at the time.

When Maggie came to the United States in 2005, she started at one of two public middle schools in the city with a SEI program. She noted the racial tensions between the non-SEI education students (most of whom were Black) and the SEI program students (most of whom were Chinese) at the school. She reflected on an incident in detail:

> There is a lot of racial tension at the school. We would get in line for lunch in the cafeteria, for instance, and some students would yell out, "Oh, Chinese this and that." When we go to use the restrooms they would beat us up. Now when someone needs to use the restroom, we would always go together so that there is always someone there. One of my friend and a Black girl once fought in the girl's restroom. The school restrooms' stalls do not have locks, and so that day a Black girl kicked my friend's stall opened and then they would splash us with water. It was really horrific. My friend tried to ignore what they were doing to us, but she had enough. She couldn't take the hostilities and discriminations that were happening to us anymore. My friend was really, really mad and so she grabbed a trashcan and threw it at the girl. My friend didn't want to hurt her so she threw the trashcan near the girl's feet. The girl threw it back at my friend and told us to "shut up" and called us "stupid people" when we spoke in Cantonese. While we only have been in the U.S. for a few months we knew what those words meant. They ended up fighting and the principal came and talked to us ... He asked us what happened and the girl and my friend both were suspended for a day because they were fighting.

These racial discriminations were similar to other research with Asian American students (Rosenbloom & Way, 2004). While the throwing incidents like the one described by Yee-Mun are not currently happening at the moment and the principal at Maggie's school suspended the girls involved in the fight, schools are not resolving the tensions since other incidents have been (re)occurring. Instead, these schools are quick fixing and heightening the issue by reinforcing the status quo. For instance, Cityview High School decided by finding an alternative route for the SEI Chinese students as they head to other parts of the school (i.e., the general education quarters) would solve all problems while suspension was the decision at Maggie's school. Rather than facilitating dialogues about human relations, the administration opted to silence the incidences and maintain segregation and misunderstanding. Such actions are minimal interventions and, more importantly, distractions from dismantling stereotypes and addressing justice and cultural competency (Kivel, 2002; Ladson-Billings, 1994, 1995a, 1995b). Schools often do not provide students the space to challenge and critique the status quo. Students are not taught to engage in critical analyses of race and intersectionality and are denied access to ethnic studies, anti-racism pedagogy, and interactions with their peers. As illustrated with the above narratives, schools need to incorporate critical and anti-racist dialogues for every member of the school community (e.g., students, school personnel, and students' families). Schools, moreover, must provide students the tools, skills, and critical analysis to challenge the status quo and create change in their schools and communities, particularly interracial and intraracial relationships. Instead of perpetuating the constant image of the demonized and angry "Black girl" or the quiet and submissive Asian, students like Maggie would begin to understand the inequalities and hierarchies (e.g., race, class, gender, and sexual orientation) in the United States through building coalition with other oppressed groups to dismantle the injustices. If such dialogues are not implemented carefully, the racial tensions, discriminations, and misunderstandings would remain or heighten even more, as we have seen from the above testimonials.

In addition to experiencing such incidents inside the school walls, the young people also expressed similar incidents beyond the schools. For example, both Joe and Calvin, who attended the same middle school but at different times, experienced continuous bullying and racial hostility on the school buses. Joe is about seven years older than Calvin, yet their experiences remained unchanged. Joe, a graduating high school senior, vividly recalled the teasing and fights taking inside the school bus in middle school.

> When we ride the school bus, the Black students would tease us. It happens almost every day but we usually don't let it bother us. We would sit in the front [of the bus] and there's a gap between the Black students and us. We don't care what they say. We just ignore them ... However, they scream at us and call us idiots and talk in a strange language, like pretending to speak Chinese. So we would fight them. They would also put lotion on our hair. At first we didn't know what it was. We thought it was white out so we fought them.

Since Joe was coming to CYC at the time, he was able to tell the staff what happened: "I talked to Wai-Ming and then she spoke with the school." Calvin, a sixth grader and twelve years old, expressed that "most of the people are mean" at his middle school because of the hostility that the Chinese students experience on the school bus. It was so bad that Calvin explained why Asian and Black students have to switch seating arrangements on the school bus:

> Now the Asian people on the bus have to sit in the back and the Black people who were in the back are in the front. The people in the back throw stuff at us ... They would throw metal spoons, pencils, bags like pencil covers. They just laugh and throw things. I bend down so they couldn't hit me ... the bus driver told the assistant principal, who said we have to switch places on the bus. However, things are still the same. Now since we sit in the back of the bus, they would trip us on purpose when we walk pass them. They would also spit and sneeze as we walk by.

When asked why the non-SEI students would do or say these things, a number of the recent immigrants and 1.5 generations noted language barrier and misunderstanding could be the reasons. In general, they made comments like the following: "When we speak Cantonese, they assume that we are saying something bad about them. We speak Cantonese all the time. That's why they do those things to us." Instead of seeing it as a larger societal matter, the youth blamed themselves for these incidents (i.e., for speaking Cantonese "all the time").

The way the recent immigrant students respond to the various incidents depends on their comfort in and understanding of English. Ka-Kay explained:

> Before when we didn't know any English we would ignore them, but as we live in the U.S. longer and understand more English, some of us would respond by swearing back at them. If we can't take it anymore, some of us would fight them. Some of the boys would get into fights because they couldn't take the hostility any longer.

The issues of race and ethnic identity along with their immigrant status are converging for recent immigrant youth. Consequently, when schools ignore the racial tensions and maintain systems of oppression and segregation, students' academic, social, and emotional well-being is deeply affected. Wayne, the child of Chinese immigrants and a graduating high school senior, went through a series of depression due to experiencing racism, discriminations, and stereotypes:

> I just don't want to go back to school. I was 11 and in middle school. I was really frustrated. I just didn't like the students there. I just don't like them making fun of me. They just keep doing it. They did verbal abuse and one of them hit me.

Through his eleven years as a Youth Worker at CYC, Jeff described immigrant and U.S. American born youth of color as constantly encountering "battlegrounds." For instance, he reflected how racism becomes a daily battleground the youth encounter in school and society:

> I mean racism is a big thing. And so being an immigrant, being an Asian kid, you get it from everyone. You get it from the Asian American kids. You get it from the Black kids. You get it from the White kids. You get it from the Latino kids. So as an immigrant, sometimes they might not even have a voice because they don't know how to express it or they don't know the language well. And that's not an easy thing at all.

The issue of exclusion, racial hostility, and invisibility in schools came up frequently and each time, the youth expressed deep emotions about such occurrences. With the racial tensions occurring at their schools, young people, like Ka-Kay, wishes "everyone in the school could all simply get along and be friends with each other, like at CYC."

Since their immigrant parents have long and inflexible work hours and since the youth view their schools as uncaring, they view community-based organizations as a safe and comfortable youth (comm)unity space. Chapters 5 and 6 illustrate the services and support that HCCC's youth program, Community Youth Center (CYC), offers to the youth, their families, and the Asian American community in the Harborview area. Chapter 5 explores the role and impact of HCCC and its youth program (CYC) in assisting and providing information, support, and advocacy for low-income and working poor Chinese immigrant families.

Works cited

Ancheta, A. N. (1998) *Race, rights, and the Asian American experience*. New Brunswick, NJ: Rutgers University Press.

Brand, D. (1987, August 31). The new whiz kids: Why Asian Americans are doing so well and what it costs them. *Time, 130*(9), 42–51.

Carter, P. L. (2005). *Keepin' it real: School success beyond black and white*. New York, NY: Oxford University Press.

Castagno, A. E. (2008). "I don't want to hear that!": Legitimating Whiteness through silence in schools. *Anthropology & Education Quarterly, 39*(3), 314–333.

Chang, B., & Au, W. (2007/2008, Winter). You're Asian, How could you fail math? Unmasking the myth of the model minority. *Rethinking Schools, 22*(2), 15–18.

Cho, S. K. (1993). Korean Americans vs. African Americans: Conflict and construction. In R. Gooding-Williams (Ed.), *Reading Rodney King/reading urban uprising* (pp. 196–211). New York, NY: Routledge.

Conchas, G. Q. (2006). *The color of success: Race and high achieving urban youth*. New York, NY: Teachers College Press.

Hussar, W. J., & Bailey, T. M. (2014). *Projections of education statistics to 2022 (NCES 2014–051)*. U.S. Department of Education, National Center for Education Statistics. Washington, DC: U.S. Government Printing Office.

Kim, E. H. (2003). Home is where the *Han* Is: A Korean-American perspective on the Los Angeles upheavals. In R. Gooding-Williams (Ed.), *Reading Rodney King/reading urban uprising* (pp. 215–235). New York, NY: Routledge.

Kivel, P. (2002). *Uprooting racism: How White people can work for racial justice* (revised ed.). Gabriola Island, BC, Canada: New Society Publishers.

Ladson-Billings, G. (1994). *Dreamkeepers: Successful teachers of African American children*. San Francisco, CA: Jossey-Bass.

Ladson-Billings, G. (1995a). But that's just good teaching! The case for culturally relevant pedagogy. *Theory Into Practice, 34*(3), 159–165.

Ladson-Billings, G. (1995b, Fall). Toward a theory of culturally relevant pedagogy. *American Educational Research Journal, 32*(3), 465–491.

Lee, S. J. (1996). *Unraveling the model minority stereotype: Listening to Asian American youth.* New York, NY: Teachers College Press.

Lee, S. J. (2001). More than "model minorities" or "delinquents": A look at Hmong American high school students. *Harvard Educational Review, 71*(3), 505–528.

Lee, S. J. (2005). *Up against Whiteness: Race, school and immigrant youth.* New York, NY: Teachers College Press.

Lew, J. (2004). The "other" story of model minorities: Korean American high school dropouts in an urban context. *Anthropology & Education Quarterly, 35*(3), 303–323.

Li, G. (2002). *"East is east, west is west"? Home literacy, culture, and schooling.* New York, NY: Peter Lang Publishing.

Li, G. (2003). Literacy, culture, and politics of schooling: Counternarratives of a Chinese Canadian family. *Anthropology & Education Quarterly, 34*(2), 184–206.

Lopez, N. (2003). *Hopeful girls, troubled boys: Race and gender disparity in urban education.* New York, NY: Routledge.

Louie, V. S. (2004). *Compelled to excel: Immigration, education, and opportunity among Chinese Americans.* Stanford, CA: Stanford University Press.

Min, P. G. (1998). *Changes and conflicts: Korean immigrant families in New York.* Boston, MA: Allyn and Bacon.

Oakes, J. (1985). *Keeping track: How schools structure inequality.* New Haven, CT: Yale University Press.

Olsen, L. (1997). *Made in America: Immigrant students in our public schools.* New York, NY: New Press.

Ore, T. E. (2003). Maintaining inequalities: Systems of oppression and privilege. In T. E. Ore (Ed.), *The social construction of difference and inequality: Race, class, gender, and sexuality* (2nd ed., pp. 182–204). New York, NY: McGraw Hill.

Phelan, P., Davidson, A. L., & Yu, H. C. (1993). Students' multiple worlds: Navigating the borders of family, peer, and the school cultures. In P. Phelan & A. L. Davidson (Eds.), *Renegotiating cultural diversity in American school* (pp. 52–88). New York, NY: Teachers College Press.

Pollock, M. (2004). *Colormute: Race talk dilemmas in an American school.* Princeton, NJ: Princeton University Press.

Roffman, J. G., Suárez-Orozco, C., & Rhodes, J. E. (2003). Facilitating positive development in immigrant youth: The role of mentors and community organizations. In F. A. Villarruel, D. F. Perkins, L. M. Borden, & J. G. Keith (Eds.), *Community youth development: Programs, policies, and practices* (pp. 90–117). Thousand Oaks, CA: Sage Publications.

Rosenbloom, S. R., & Way, N. (2004). Experiences of discrimination among African American, Asian American, and Latino adolescents in an urban high school. *Youth and Society, 35*(4), 420–451.

Suárez-Orozco, C., & Suárez-Orozco, M. M. (2001). *Children of immigration.* Cambridge, MA: Harvard University Press.

Suárez-Orozco, C., Suárez-Orozco, M. M., & Todorova, I. (2008). *Learning a new land: Immigrant students in American society.* Cambridge, MA: Harvard University Press.

Valdés, G. (1996). *Con respecto: Bridging the distances between culturally diverse families and schools.* New York, NY: Teachers College Press.

Valdés, G. (2001). *Learning and not learning English: Latino students in American schools.* New York, NY: Teachers College Press.

Valenzuela, A. (1999). *Subtractive schooling: U.S.-Mexican youth and the politics of caring.* Albany, NY: State of New York Press.

Wing, L. C. (1971–1974). *Sojourner I, II, III, IV.* Asian Writers Project. Berkeley, CA: Berkeley Unified School District.

Wong, N. W. A. (2008). "They see us as resource": The role of a community-based youth center in supporting the academic lives of low-income Chinese American Youth. *Anthropology & Education Quarterly, 39*(2), 181–204.

Wong, N. W. A. (2010). "Cuz they care about the people who goes there": The multiple roles of a community-based youth center in providing "Youth (Comm)Unity" for low-income Chinese American youth. *Urban Education, 45*(5), 708–739.

CHAPTER FIVE

Accessing information, opportunities, and advocacy

Mrs. Liao works at a factory that makes crab rangoons, egg rolls, meatballs, and chicken wings for local area restaurants. Her day starts at 5:30 in the morning and she does not get home until 7 or 8 o'clock at night. She was "extremely motivated" to learn English and thus she enrolled in HCCC's Adult ESL class. However, after five weeks, Mrs. Liao stopped attending because she was having "a really hard time grasping it." Due to her long work hours, Mrs. Liao is unable to attend and participate in many of her daughters' educational events. Nevertheless, she enjoys listening to their day-to-day stories. She explained, "My daughters tell me they can communicate with peers and the staffs at CYC really easily. They can ask people for homework help and take English classes ... They find the staff members to be really caring and have a lot of patience." Through these stories, she views HCCC and CYC as "a good place" for her daughters and the community. Mrs. Liao highlights how HCCC serves as a "bridge" for adults, children, and youth in the community.

> CYC, and HCCC as a whole, is a very resourceful place in Chinatown for recent immigrants to bridge with U.S. society. For instance, when my daughters first came to the U.S., they didn't know a word of English and didn't have any friends. CYC is a good way for them to meet people and to learn English ... My daughters always tell me how good of a place CYC is; therefore, I would then tell my friends who have teenage children about CYC.

Other parents, such as Mr. and Mrs. Mui, also shared similar sentiments. Mrs. Mui explained, "As you know, being low-income and recent immigrants, we always need to work long hours; and thus my husband and I really want our daughter to do different activities in a safe place like CYC. I don't want our daughter to feel unsafe, depressed, and lonely."

Through building *and* maintaining a sense of trust and dialogue with the youth and their families, individuals, like the Liao's and Mui's, would recommend CYC to their own networks. The students and parents, who identified the U.S. school system as difficult to navigate and negotiate, find the services and support at CBOs, like HCCC, valuable because they understand and acknowledge their family background. Moreover, as I have noted in Chapters 3 and 4, the youth and their parents in this research for the most part found the U.S. school system inaccessible. Scholars such as Lew (2003) found that since teachers and guidance counselors were unable to assist the students with academic and employment opportunities, the youth turned to after-school tutors and counselors in their Korean American community. Similarly, Mrs. Liao viewed CYC and HCCC as a visible and important resource since the staff members were able to connect and build trust with the people that they serve *and* understand how to negotiate the dominant society (Delpit, 1988, 1995). The families were able to find information, advocacy, and support from CYC and HCCC.

My research challenges the dangers of parent education programs to argue that, through listening, respecting, and understanding the community's needs, HCCC offers cultural relevant and holistic family education programs. By using a cultural relevant approach, rather than a cultural deficit approach of blaming the family, the parents viewed HCCC workshops to be insightful. Additionally, as I have stated elsewhere (Wong, 2008):

> [B]y maintaining an ongoing communication with the youth and their families, CYC is viewed as a visible resource because the staff are connected with the community and had often acquired the information, skills, and social capital to successfully negotiate the dominant society. Thus, parents [and the youth] know where to go if they ever need assistance. (p. 193)

Through embracing the families' cultural wealth, maintaining trust with the youth, families, and community, and having a positive caring presence, CYC serves as a welcoming space for the community. Thus, youth and parents know where to go if they need assistance. For instance, youth and adults regularly visited HCCC to meet one-on-one with the staffs. Additionally, many of the youth and parents expressed they would introduce others in their ethnic networks, such as a family member or friend to HCCC and CYC. Or they heard about HCCC through their families, friends, and teachers.

Maggie, a freshman in high school who came to the United States almost two years ago at age fourteen, explains the resources that CYC offered her and other children of immigrants:

> Being recent immigrants, we would never go out on our own, because we didn't speak English and so we were scared of asking people for directions. And so coming to CYC changed all that because they were able to help us with everything. For instance, we didn't know a lot of the different places in the city. They would take us to all the different museums, the aquarium, malls and tell us what these places are and what's inside. Before we were afraid to go alone or as a group. CYC exposed us to these different places that we never heard of before.

As I will illustrate in this chapter, CYC and HCCC serve as a triangulated bridge as the youth and their immigrant parents try to navigate the dominant U.S. culture and, at the same time, they try to understand each other and themselves. HCCC and CYC play a dual role in helping low-income and working-class Chinese American young people *and* their immigrant parents bridge the intergenerational gap between the two. CYC also helps the youth and their families negotiate a system that is unfamiliar and transparent for them. In doing so, CYC links the three worlds or "multiple worlds" (Phelan, Davidson, & Yu, 1991, 1993, 1998). I suggest CYC offers young people and their families the codes, or rules, needed to access and navigate the "culture of power" (Delpit, 1988, 1995), while also honoring and upholding their community cultural wealth. Delpit (1995) explains:

> [W]e must take the responsibility to *teach*, to provide for students who do not already possess them, the additional codes of power. But I also do not believe that we should teach students to passively adopt an alternate code. They must be encouraged to understand the value of the code they already possess as well as to understand the power realities in this country. (p. 40)

These codes are necessary because, as Delpit argues, those who have power have established and maintained a hegemonic culture. While Delpit focused on the need for teachers and schools to teach these codes, I will illustrate how low-income Chinese American youth and their immigrant families are able to acquire them from CBOs, like CYC. Thus, the youth embrace code-switching throughout their lives (Christensen, 2009; Delpit, 2009).

As noted earlier, all of the youth were introduced to CYC through their social networks, such as a family members, friends, or school personnel (Lew, 2003; Louie, 2004). And once they are here, the reciprocal process continues where they start telling their friends and family networks about CYC. For instance, Cindy explained how many of the youth were introduced to CYC:

We've established a really good reputation and as a result, parents and youth would let others know about our center. When a parent comes in, we asked them how they heard about us they would say so and so told us about CYC. I think we've established a really good reputation in the community. As a result, parents and youth would let others know about our center.

Louie (2004) noted the importance of ethnic networks for the Chinese American "respondents" in her research where "their parents had relied on such networks" to understand the public school system in New York City (p. 89).

Below, I provide examples of how children of immigrants and their families were able to obtain information, access, skills, and advocacy. The following experiences of youth, parents, and staffs provide a glimpse into how CYC provides the youth and their families with understanding the dominant culture while maintaining their cultural wealth.

Parents obtaining information and resources

As I have mentioned in Chapter 3, parents found navigating and negotiating the U.S. schools to be difficult. While schools and the dominant culture often placed the responsibility on parents and families to understand the U.S. school system themselves, those from immigrant backgrounds and low-income households are at a great disadvantage. Kwak (2003) states that having an "extensive social support from [ones] own-ethnic network helps to keep family relations closer" (p. 132). Intergenerational conflict also is often a normative concern in immigrant families. Some research indicates immigrant families that support the strategy of accommodation without assimilation, or selective acculturation, encounter fewer conflicts (Gibson, 1988; Lee, 2005; Portes & Rumbaut, 2001). For instance, Gibson (1988) found the strategy of *accommodation without assimilation* was important for Punjabi Sikhs in California. In this chapter, I will illustrate how HCCC is able to bridge the intergenerational gaps between the children, their immigrant parents, and U.S. schools.

The parents in my research were able to find the advocacy, information, and support at CBOs like HCCC. By developing and maintaining a sense of trust and understanding with parents and youth, HCCC and CYC was able to offer workshops and one-on-one meetings to the community. Far too often the purpose of parent and family education programs is to change families; and by doing so, there is a great danger of force assimilation and destroying family worldviews. According to Valdés (1996), while these programs attempt to find solutions to break the cycle of school failure, "[t]he problem is that they are seeking to break the cycle by focusing exclusively on one explanation for the poor school performance of non-mainstream youngsters" (p. 195). Thus, they are subscribing to existing assumptions of power and fail to consider how inequalities affect schooling outcomes. Many of the teachers in Valdés' study fail to see and value the community cultural wealth of the Mexican immigrant families. While Valdés suggests there are dangers to parent programs, we should focus on the assets that immigrant families bring with them. This study challenges the dangers of parent education programs to argue that HCCC and CYC offer culturally relevant parent education programs.

Previously, I explained the significance of CYC's holistic and collaborative model with the youths' families: "The longevity of CYC's approach and model is due to years of building and maintaining respect and trust with youth *and* adults" (Wong, 2013, p. 167). HCCC and CYC, therefore, serve as an accessible and welcoming space for immigrant parents and their children to obtain academic and social support and resources. In the past, the staffs expressed how parents expected the staff to "teach" their children for them. Cindy explained in detail the importance of collaborating with parents, family, and school in order to provide a holistic teaching approach rather than CYC being the sole responsible:

> Parents' view of CYC is that it is a very safe place for their child to go to. It is also a place where their child can do their homework and receive tutoring. At the same time, a lot of the parents expected us to hold a lot of responsibilities. This was what I experienced before but I don't really see it that as much now. Before when I called the parents, they would always tell me to talk to their child for them and to teach them … Parents think their child doesn't listen to them because they would tell us that "we tell them all the time but they don't listen to us." As a result, they think maybe someone else teaching their child then they would listen … This was what I've experienced before. We've been telling parents that we need to work together and so their views have changed … We don't believe that we are the only ones; rather it includes the parents, the school, and us. We have to always remember that we need to work together because we can't do it all on our own. So it's not just the Community Youth Center … The point is we all need to work together.

In response to working together with parents and family, CYC and the Family Support program regularly hold workshops for youth, parents, and family members in the community. The staff members conducted phone outreach to parents to inform and invite them about the events as well as mailed out bilingual fliers. Parents who attended the workshops gave high remarks to the information they have learned. Some of the workshop topics included maintaining strong parent–child relationships, knowing your rights at schools, special education policies, and mental health issues. These types of information function as social capital since parents were able to gain knowledge of the dominant culture and access the public school system. For instance, Ms. Chan attended a few of the workshops and the open house at HCCC and CYC. One in particular she remembered vividly:

> We learned about the school system in Harborview and parent-child communica-
> tions. Wai-Ming [CYC director at the time] and the Family Support coordinator ran
> these workshops. I found the workshops helpful because I was able to understand and
> follow along especially since they were in Cantonese.

The workshop series highlighted the facilitative role of CYC and HCCC. For instance, CYC's open house was an opportunity for parents and families to meet the staff, to learn (more) about the services offered at CYC, and obtain information about the U.S. public school system. Heather, a Youth Worker, elaborated:

> The purpose of the open house was to provide parents more information about what
> their child is doing at CYC during ESL Classes and the Tutoring Program. It also
> gave the parents a chance to ask staff any questions they have in regards to our pro-
> gram and certain exam, such as the elite public high school entrance test and the state
> mandated exam.

The staffs developed the agenda based on their experiences working with the young people and the suggestions from the youth and parents. Cindy, the Tutoring Coordinator, stated in detail:

> Mainly, we feel that most parents lack the knowledge of school testing; therefore, we
> included [Harborview's and the other public school districts in the area's] required
> exams and testing dates. We also included SAT, SAT II and TOEFL info. We also
> mentioned CYC's programs.

Mr. Mui remembered "the staffs told us about CYC and what things they offered like sports, activities, tutoring, ESL classes and different fieldtrips." Knowing many family members in the community work in ethnic restaurants and businesses, the event was held during the day of the week when many families had the day off. In sum, CYC's understanding and respect for the community is reflected when events are held.

The parents whom I interviewed expressed coming to the CYC Open House was "very informative" and "important" because they were not aware of U.S. school practices and policies (Wong, 2013). Mrs. Lau noted:

> The workshops were really helpful. I learned a lot of things. Other parents found it
> very helpful as well. For instance, we didn't know what the SATs and elite public high
> school entrance test were. We now understand them, like when the child needs to take
> them, if there is a fee to the exams, and if so, how much does each cost. Attending

these workshops really, really helped the parents, because we just didn't know any of these things before. The staff explained everything in great detail and clarity. They are very dedicated and passionate with what they do. The parents really enjoyed coming to these workshops.

Another parent, Mrs. Liao, echoed parallel sentiments:

I learned numerous things from attending the open house. ...Before this event, I never heard of the SAT and didn't know what it was. ... They informed families about the different tests that our children will be taking and suggested when and how many times they should be taking the SATs. I found this information to be beneficial. I consider CYC a good place so I always encourage my children to go there.

Mr. Mui, likewise, found the open house to be "very informative," particularly learning about the U.S. educational system: "I am more knowledgeable about the U.S. school system after attending the event." As mentioned in Chapter 3, the Mui family was separated for five years due to immigration. As a result, while Mrs. Mui was in the United States, Mr. Mui took care of their daughter, Betty, and was able to help her with homework and understood the education system in China. Although Mr. and Mrs. Mui were able to assist Betty with her schooling in China, they now felt "lost" and "overwhelmed" trying to navigate through the U.S. school system. As a result, Mr. Mui considered the services at CYC crucial for his family:

It was helpful that the staffs were able to inform us and explain what these things were. For example, the staffs spoke to us about the different services that are available at the CYC. They also shared with us the different tests that our children will be taking in school, like what they were and when they will be taking these exams. They told us about the school entrance exam because a lot of the parents didn't even know what these things were. We were able to gain more knowledge about our children's schooling. If I hadn't attended the open house, then I wouldn't have known these things. That's why it's important for me to attend. For instance, if we didn't know about these exams then we wouldn't be able to help our daughter. We were able to find services that can help her practice and improve on these exams.

Similar to other parents, Mr. Mui expressed a deep interest in attending more CYC events in the future:

I am definitely interested in attending more events in the future because it's valuable information. It's good to have a better understanding of what goes on at my daughter's school and with her education. In general, the parents all had positive comments about the open house. I am glad that I attended. I'd gained a better understanding of my daughter's schooling now.

At the same time, Mr. Mui, as well as other parents, noted schools' limited interactions with immigrant families. He suggested that schools should communicate more with families since a sense of "disconnect" often occurs between families and schools. Mr. Mui explained:

> Schools should notify parents about these different exams and any upcoming events and information because, as immigrant parents, we are not aware of these things. We learned about these requirements and information by attending the CYC Open House. Therefore, if we hadn't attended the events at CYC, we wouldn't have known any of these things. That's why it was useful for us to attend.

Overall, parents and families gained valuable information about the U.S. school system. In particular, they learned about the pubic schools and how to guide and support their children in preparing for the various tests (Wong, 2013).

In addition to informing parents and family members about CYC and the public school systems in the area, some of the CYC youth performed a skit about parent–child communication and relationships at the open house. Cindy explained the importance of the skit:

> Over the years, staffs witnessed the ineffective communications between the youth and their parents. Therefore, we developed the skit on "positive and negative ways in communicating with your child."

"[T]he parents all had a great insightful experience," reflected Cindy. The parents who I spoke with also had positive comments about the skit. Mrs. Lau reflected on what she learned:

> As parents, we shouldn't always tell and force our children to "always study, always study". We shouldn't yell at them and pressure them to learn all these different things. Rather it is important for parents to find out what their interests are. If they are interested in doing an activity, then we should consider letting them try it. Pressuring them too much doesn't work. … For instance, the skit performed by the youth was about a father and son. The father wouldn't let the son watch that much T.V. and told the son to do a lot of different things. It was good to see the skit from a different angle. We see how there are parents who are really strict and others who are more carefree with their children.

She said her husband found the open house to be particularly educational and informative and appreciated attending these events:

> After the open house, my husband used those tips. He found the tips to be really helpful because he didn't realize he was doing and saying certain things to our children before. After several weeks, seems like he is going back to his old self and so I tell him he needs to go back to CYC more often. [Laughs]

As Mrs. Lau explained, they were able to observe and analyze parent–child communication from a different point of view that was respectful and relevant. In doing so, the Laus appreciated the skit and enhanced their relationship with their children (Wong, 2013).

Since the creation of the Family Support program in 2005, the coordinator has been facilitating all of the parent/family workshops while still maintaining communication with the different HCCC program coordinators and staffs. Each of the program staffs would outreach to and inform the families in their programs. Each year, the family support coordinator would organize six to ten parent workshops and forums. All of the workshops were held at HCCC and the majority was free. One of the workshop series, which ran for five weeks in early 2008, focused on special education and was facilitated by a bilingual Chinese American professor from the local four-year public university. Its purpose was to increase parent and family's knowledge of special education (e.g., current laws and parents' rights). Another focused on communication strategies for parents with teenagers. Mrs. Wu, Calvin's mom, recalled attending the parent–child communication workshop that the Family Support Coordinator facilitated being relevant:

> [T]hey invited experts and all of the information were relevant and practical. They mentioned parents should spend more time with their children and create different educational activities like reading book logs. They suggested giving your child stars after they finished a book. Then give them an award after reaching a number of stars. Calvin liked the idea. I like it, too, and agree with what they said. However, my work schedule became increasingly busy. I didn't have time. Then he had too much homework and I didn't have enough time so we stopped. I hope to revisit it soon. Overall, I found the workshops very helpful.

For the past few months, because of Mrs. Wu's demanding 12-hour day work schedule, she is no longer able to attend the workshops.

Ms. Chan attended a similar workshop, because she was experiencing "difficulty communicating with her youngest son due to a language barrier" (Wong, 2013, p. 170). She explained their disconnection:

> He speaks English and I speak Cantonese. Sometimes he would say, "Mom, you don't even understand what I am trying to say." I would tell him "you should keep telling me until I understand it." When he was younger, he would show me the words using the Chinese electronic dictionary, but now he wouldn't because he thinks it's annoying. It's hard because sometimes he can't express and explain in Cantonese what he wants to say to me and I can't do the same in English.

As research has shown, in many immigrant households a child's relationships with their parents and elders often become quite alienated and distant, particularly during the child's teenage years (Qin, 2006). These relationships are further complicated by the fact that children of immigrants frequently pick up U.S. culture sooner than their parents (Lee & Kumashiro, 2005; Qin, 2006; Suárez-Orozco & Suárez-Orozco, 2001; Sung, 1987; Wong, 2013). As a result, the CYC workshop aimed to offer resources and provide families support and opportunities to share their experiences.

Ms. Chan found the workshop to be "extremely important." After attending the workshop, rather than "blaming" herself for the intergenerational gap with her youngest son, Ms. Chan learned that communication takes time and commitment and it is an ongoing process. She explained:

> It can't happen immediately. Instead, you need to build that relationship. Then the process would slowly change and communication would improve. Now, my communication with my son has gradually improved.

Mrs. Wong similarly stated, "I am still learning how to have better communication with my son. I am still learning and finding out ways to do so." As I have shown, parents found HCCC workshops to be a vital resource and were open to learning about topics that ranged from the U.S. public school system to parent–child relationships.

All of the parents who attended HCCC workshops expressed great interest in attending more in the future. Some of the parents specifically spoke about the fear that their communication and relationship with their child(ren) would deteriorate as they got older. As a result, they would like to attend more workshops that could assist and support parents through this process. For instance, when Mrs. Lau suggested some topics for future workshops, she noted "it would be good to talk about our children's education and CYC updates" because "parents would like to know what is happening in their children's lives." When I asked her to elaborate, she explained, "Right now, they [the children] would still tell us things, so we know what is happening. However, I don't know in the future when they are older if they would still maintain an open communication with us." Another parent also expressed parallel thoughts. She recalled her middle school-aged son had always told her and her husband about any upcoming school events. For instance, they attended their son's school basketball game several times last year. However, this year, "he doesn't tell us things anymore. He doesn't want us to go to his school now," she explained. The school recently held a parent–teacher conference and an open house earlier in the school year, but "he didn't want us to go to them." At the time of the interview, they were increasingly struggling to understand their child:

> Maybe he's older now, so that's why he feels embarrassed because we don't know English. We can't communicate with the teachers. We have a lot of questions, but we don't know how to communication with the teachers. So that's why he doesn't really want us to go.

In general, parents enjoyed attending the various HCCC workshops. Through these workshops, parents were able to access and obtain valuable information about the public schools in the area, U.S. higher education, CYC's services, and parent–child relationships. Therefore, the families in this community were able to gain more confidence about U.S. public schools and other institutions because "CYC involved the entire family, was aware of how obscured the dominant discourses are, and at the same time was able to honor [the families'] cultural wealth" (Wong, 2013, p. 171). CYC and HCCC served a facilitative role in supporting and working with low-income and working class immigrant families through cultural relevant and holistic programming.

"The staffs are like stars": Youth accessing information, skills, and opportunities

In addition to providing services and support for parents, HCCC offers services and support for children and young people. For middle and high school young people, CYC is where "you can improve oneself … like your skills," said Allyson, a second generation Chinese American and a ninth grader, "when I went to the art club, I got better at drawing. So it is a place to improve your skills." She explained that the different clubs and programs are helpful for young people: "You know how there's ESL class here, like people can improve their English and writing. There's sports and tutoring as well." Equally important, CYC is a place that brings young people together "to help one another, like tutoring and I got help with drawing. I got better at it," noted Allyson. As I will illustrate below and in the following chapters, reciprocal learning and teaching occur among the youth and staff, staff and their colleagues, and youth and their peers at CYC.

It is important to note that at least a handful of young people had no internet access, printer, and/or computer at home. If they have a computer, for instance, it is an older model. As a result, many young people find the resources at CYC to be important. Philip, a second generation and graduating high school senior, uses the computers at CYC for research and other homework purposes because his "computer at home is really, really old that we needed to fix it several times already." As a result, CYC is a place where Philip and the other young people have access to technologies. Additionally, with the high cost of rent in Harborview, particularly in Chinatown, many low-income immigrant families could only afford a one-bedroom apartment, which ranges from $850 to more than $1,000. The lack of space, as a result, affected the youth. While CYC's space is not huge, it is accessible especially since Chinatown does not have a public library branch location. For Becky, who we met in Chapter 4, CYC is "a place do my homework." Becky explained how she approaches her school assignments since she does not have internet access and a printer at home:

> I have a computer at home but we don't have internet so I can't go online to conduct research. So if the assignment is due on Monday then I need to do it two days earlier. I would use the computer and printer at CYC. I make sure I have all of the things I need before CYC closes on Friday … I feel bad because every time I come here and do my homework I need to print things out, usually articles and pictures. Every time I print out something it always run out of paper. I feel bad.

Young people, who do not have access to technology, were able to obtain such services at CYC. As a result, CBOs are places to access opportunities, resources, and information, which I will illustrate in detail below.

CYC's clubs serving as opportunities

The CYC clubs provide opportunities to gain knowledge and build trust. "The clubs are very youth work focused," noted Erin, the ESL teacher, "which is letting the youth make a lot of the decisions, letting them do things, empowering them to do things." Some of the clubs such as cooking and band are offered year-round at CYC. Cindy echoed similar sentiments:

> The purpose of the clubs is for them to develop different hands-on experience and skills. We just don't want to focus on academics all the time, but we believe in a balance. It's different skills that they learn, such as life survival skills. Learning how to cook will develop them to be more independent and lead a healthy lifestyle. And a lot of the skills like knitting they might not have the opportunity to learn from their parents because they're at work.

In other words, CYC understands the importance of not solely focusing on academics but providing different outlets and opportunities for young people to experience different activities in a relaxed and nonhigh stakes setting. They also understand the youths' family background—their parents working long hours, from low-income and working class immigrant families—in order to better serve the community as a whole.

There are a number of youth who are at home by themselves in the evenings because their parents are at work. As a result, Cindy explained the importance of the cooking club, which meets twice a week for an hour each time:

> It's a skill for them to learn. I mean knowing the fact that a lot of our teens their parents are very busy. They might be home by themselves and they might have an instant

noodle and things like that but it's not healthy. So we teach them simple recipes and also about culture. In the past, I tried to do international food and we did recipes. It's learning about other cultures as well.

While I was at CYC, the youth made a variety of dishes, with assistance from a staff. Some of the food included: taco, Vietnamese vegetarian soup, pasta with red sauce, seasoned baked chicken, and pizza. They would often bring a stack of cards (e.g., Uno or game cards) with them because the staffs and youth would play games as they waited for the food to cook. As a result, clubs are opportunities for youth and staffs to build and maintain trust. I composed the following field note from one of the cooking days:

> It was almost 3 p.m. and shortly after one of the youth signed in, Jeff asked about ten youth "are you ready?" I wasn't sure what Jeff meant. They all said "yea" and began to get items from the shelves that are above the sink: pasta, canned tomato, grounded pepper, aluminum foil, etc. At first, I thought they were cleaning the shelves, but I realized they were getting ready to cook when they took the materials and a stack of Uno cards, and headed out the door. Jeff told Erin that they were going upstairs [to the kitchen]. At around 4 p.m., the cooking group returned with a large pot covered with aluminum foil. The aroma of tomato sauce slowly emerges when Jeff lifted the aluminum foil from the pot. He then asked if anyone wanted pasta. Immediately, everyone, especially the middle school youth, answered "yes!" With their glowing smiles they lined up behind Jeff. The scene reminded me of a summer afternoon when young children hear and see an ice-cream truck coming around the block. The youth were waiting patiently, but at the same time eagerly with huge smiles on their face as they try to peek through Jeff, who was putting the pasta into small bowls. The youth who made the dish would hand it out to those in line. A few minutes later, some of the youth asked if they could have seconds once they finished. (field notes, February 6, 2007)

With the everlasting budget cuts facing public schools, particular in urban and rural areas, many students often do not have the option of a holistic curriculum. As a result the resources available for students who attend low-income and urban and rural school districts are at a huge disadvantage. CBOs such as CYC are crucial in order to provide young people a musical outlet. Peter and Wai-Ming started the youth band, which began as a guitar club. Peter was a guitar and drums instructor in Hong Kong and played in a band. In the beginning, Peter led a group of about six CYC youth in the guitar club. He explained the importance of having music in young people's lives:

> I believe that music is a good way for teens to open up their minds. Through music, they can have a better understanding of themselves and others. For instance, in band you need to have good and strong communication skills and teamwork. We try to

build these skills for the youth here. And then music is a form of art. Sometimes it's not just about studying. They can learn about another art form to build up their creativity and decide how they could do things in the future.

The young people who were a part of the guitar club and later the CYC band spoke positively about their experience and Peter's role. Joe, a graduating high school senior, decided to join the guitar club because he wanted to "learn something new" and found out Peter was teaching. Joe shared some of his experiences:

> The club started the summer of my eighth grade. Peter's personality is similar to mines. He's funny, outgoing, talks a lot, and turns everything enjoyable. When we started band, he taught me how to play the drums. He taught me how to be serious cuz I would usually fool around a lot and every time I practiced the results are not that good, because we don't have unity. He taught me how to feel the music like the beats. He told us to listen to more songs and each time we listen we feel the beats of the song.

Later when the guitar club grew into the CYC youth band, more members joined, which consisted of a drummer, bass player, guitarist, keyboardist, and singers. They performed annually at HCCC and CYC events, such as Asian Pacific Islander American Heritage Month, banquets, shows, etc. Today, the CYC band has grown into a multilevel band. Those who are more experienced would mentor others with their instruments, beats, and music sheets. Anna, who was a part of the CYC band for five years, recalls the "older teens would teach the younger teens. We would come together to practice. The one-on-one time was a system that Peter developed." After he left CYC as a full-time staff, Peter was hired as a contracted consultant and came to CYC once a week to run the youth bands, which he did for two years. The youth decided to have a special sendoff and appreciation performance for Peter that included Cantonese MCing, singing, live band, and hip-hop dance performances. The following excerpt is from the field notes I wrote that day:

> It was a Friday night in late-March. The evening breeze began to settle in. The CYC band and the hip-hop dance club are performing in tonight's CYC Asian Nite, which is a free and open to the community. The program is scheduled for 6 to 8p.m. All week, the young people expressed this will be Peter's last week and thus they wanted to do something special for him. When I was at CYC for my research in 2005, Peter naturally interacted with the young people. He brings so much laughter to their youthful faces that their stresses are erased during their time at CYC. All afternoon, the young people were taking the equipment to Hope Elementary School's auditorium for this evening's show. They made at least six trips. A few hours earlier, performers were having a run-through of their songs, dance routine, MCing, and the technicians were setting up and adjusting the stage (e.g., lighting, sounds, and equipment).

After talking with some of the youth organizers, I entered the auditorium and lights were blinking which signals the show was about to start. The MCs, who were all part of CYC a few years ago, stood by the doors. As I went to find a seat, a packed auditorium of K-12 school age young people, adults and elders settled into their seats. The night reminded me of Hong Kong's TVB variety entertainment shows. The singers with the band in the background sang new and old Cantonese and Mandarin pop songs. As I listened to the songs by various Hong Kong artists (e.g., Anita Mui, Eason Chan, Alan Tam, and Beyond), I quickly reminisce about my childhood memories of watching concerts on karaoke sing-alongs. The atmosphere felt like attending a live concert—glow sticks sparkling and people laughing, waving their arms in the air and singing along to songs. Some of the young children were even dancing along the aisles. Peter also came on stage and performed a couple of songs with his band. The diverse age group was really welcoming. There was definitely a sense of intergenerational unity and love that filled the auditorium. It was truly an unforgettable event that the youth did for Peter. (field notes, March 23, 2007)

In addition, youth are able to access different opportunities through CYC. For example, some of the events included attending the local MLB home game that a local funder donated. Seven youth (three female and four male) attended along with Erin and me. For four of the youth, this was their first baseball game; and thus, we were explaining the rules of the game to them. We were given a tour of the stadium, which was especially memorable for the other three youth who were huge fans, and each received a $20 food voucher. Other events included an Asian American young women conference that Erin and I brought a group of students to. The conference's mission is to empower Asian American high school and college young women. One of the workshops for high school students that day was about higher education where the panelists shared their experiences. Sarah reflected on the workshop:

They talked about their lives and colleges and how not to over stress yourself. I guess stress is something that comes to you that you're gonna get in college even if you don't want it. They tell you how to overcome it a little bit like try to pace yourself and time yourself, which was good to hear.

The keynote speaker was Helen Zia, an award-winning journalist and community activist. The exciting part was when we were having a small discussion about who Helen Zia is. After I told them, they were speechless and glad that they were able to meet and listen to her talk. We were even able to take a group photo with Helen Zia, which the youth enjoyed. After the conference, Erin and I decided to show the documentary "Who Killed Vincent Chin?" at CYC because Helen Zia was one of the key organizers demanding justice for the hate-crime. Vincent Chin, a Chinese American, was beaten to death in 1982 in the Detroit, Michigan, by two White men because they assumed Vincent was Japanese. His murder is often considered the start of a pan-ethnic Asian American movement. Also, since a lot of the young people expressed experiencing racial hostility in their schools, they needed to see how their personal experiences of racial hostility connected to the larger picture of race in the United States. As discussed in Chapter 4, they generally do not have such space in their schools to engage in dialogue and move toward actions. One of the youth reflected on their experience of the conference and watching the documentary:

> I met Helen Zia at the conference and you showed me the documentary on Vincent Chin … It was interesting, like what happened to Vincent Chin. You know how he was killed with a bat and then the people didn't get arrested after killing him. This event brought the Asians together, closer. I learned more about Asians in America at CYC cuz I don't really know much about that. Schools should teach us more because most of the time we learn about White people's history. Asians are included but most of the times they are included during wars like when the U.S. fought with Japan and when one of the presidents went to visit China. Well my teacher, he talked about how the train tracks in California were mostly made by the Chinese but it wasn't in the book. He told us. And he told us about the Gold Rush how it attracted more people to the U.S. and stuff. That's it. I never knew that much about Asian Americans until you showed us in those two workshops.[1]

This young person also noted the schools silencing the experiences of Asian Americans. The lack of culturally relevant curriculum appears to be absent in the youths' schools.

In general, young people repeatedly said, "[CYC] gave me a lot of opportunities" or CYC "opened up new things for me." Bebe elaborated:

> Today, I went to the luncheon with Jeff and three other youth. It was at the Boys and Girls' Club. CYC received a check and we were invited to go. Jeff called and asked if we would like to go. Also, I was able to volunteer at the HCCC's annual "banquet." I never attended a "banquet" before and so it was really fun to experience something like that. I learned a lot of things and I saw a lot of things as well, such as the silent auction. I wouldn't get the opportunity to volunteer at a banquet so I thought this was a good opportunity and am glad that I attended.

The information and opportunities that the young people achieve through CYC are critical since the dominant discourse either places the responsibility on the youth to find out for themselves or hides the information and opportunities. Kevin, who was seventeen years old, noted the resources and advocacy of the CYC staff in serving the youth:

> The staffs here are like stars in the night that illuminate the child to reach their potential. The staffs interact with the youth and give confidence to the youth to grow

up with respect and confidence, and be happy. The staffs have done a very good job in doing different workshops to definitely help them feel comfortable.

Providing access to higher education: Serving as counselors and mentors

While parents see higher education as necessary for their children to live a stable life, they lacked the necessary resources. Immigrant parents are unable to "help them translate those aspirations into reality" (Louie, 2004, p. 95). As a result, Asian American students from low-income and working-class families tend to feel that they are on their own in navigating through the U.S. educational system (Lee, 2005; Lew, 2003; Louie, 2004). Louie (2004) challenges the notion that class and social context do not matter for upward mobility and education. She explains:

> Due to their parents' lack of time, little English-language facility, low levels of educational attainment, and lack of exposure to American schools, working-class children believe they must navigate their school lives without much help from parents. They feel they must rely on their own abilities with regard to homework, course selection, and the college application process. (p. 101)

For example, Ming's parents always expected him and his older brother to go to college, but his parents do not know what the process entails:

> My parents tell me to work hard and get into a good college. However, they never told me what I needed to do, like the actual information of what I should be doing. They tell me I need to work hard but you need to tell me why. If I don't know what the purposes are and what the process involves then why would I do them? I didn't know what college is like. Basically I need motivation and purposes.

A lot of the youth expressed uncertainty about what college would be like. Comments such as "I had no clue where to start" were common when the topic of higher education came up. Some of the youth expressed interest in pharmacy. When I shared with them the years that it takes to complete a pharmacy degree, they were shocked about the process. Moreover, the majority of the youth were really interested when I shared my undergraduate and graduate experiences with them.

With CYC's assistance, the youth are able to better negotiate and navigate higher education. For instance, the staffs organized a free college workshop where invited speakers talked about applying to college, the financial aid applications, college interviews, and life in college, as well as arranged for campus visits to local colleges and universities. Topics included, for instance, the different types of colleges and universities, how to choose a college, and financial aid options and process. Amy, who was entering her second year in college, recalled the help she received from the CYC staff when she was going through the college process:

> CYC helped me a lot when I was applying to college, especially with my college essays. I was so stressed out. I hated the process. Even now I am so glad I am done with it. Jeff and Wai-Ming helped me. Wai-Ming told me to start doing the applications earlier cuz I'll be very busy … I started writing my essays and went through the old applications during the summer of my senior year and to see what are they looking for, like what kind of essays are they asking me to write and kinda start writing from scratch. I did everything and they helped me correct the mistakes and what else I am missing from the package, which was really helpful, too, because I won't know what else that I need.

A year later, CYC began offering a higher education mentoring program where high school juniors and seniors were paired with a mentor, which I will illustrate in Chapter 7.

Additionally, the youth found the college information they obtained at CYC were a lot more valuable than their high schools. Sarah compared the college information she received from Erin, a CYC staff, to her own high school, where things were done last minute and often shortened versions:

> Erin is very informative, especially about the future, like colleges and everything. She took me to conferences and college tours. She told me she was going to have a tour of this college and I thought that was a really great opportunity cuz that was a school I was aiming for. Plus there was free food. But with my school, they always do things very last minute. Like today, I had something about PSAT. I had 15 minutes total of the meeting cuz one of the guidance counselors, who was going to do that with us, had to go to a meeting so we only got 15 minutes. It's supposed to prepare you for the PSAT for next year, but it was cut short.

On a typical day at CYC, many of the high school youth, staff members, and I would talk about different aspects of higher education like loans, scholarships, different majors and career options, and the various types of higher institutions. The staff members would also share their college experiences. Many high school youth would come in and ask the CYC staffs and me to read over their scholarship and admission essays or ask questions about the stacks of forms that the youth need to fill out. In other words, CYC helps the youth understand the college application process, since their parents do not have the resources and schools seem to be unwilling or unable to provide them with the support. Thus, CYC plays multiple roles for the youth. In addition to providing information and opportunities for the youth, CYC also negotiates with the schools on behalf of the youth and their families, which I will now turn to.

Negotiating with schools: Serving as advocates

Both the youth and parents expressed they often ask the CYC staffs for assistance, especially questions relating to the U.S. educational system. Parents were comfortable contacting the staffs because "they are all very responsible and welcoming to our family." Mrs. Wong, whose son had been coming to CYC for over four years, noted, "The staffs are extremely committed to helping the young people as well as the recent immigrants. They are really good people." She explained her interactions with the CYC staffs:

> Sometimes my son's school would call me. When this happens, I would let Wai-Ming know. I would tell her that the teachers from Joe's school called me but I didn't understand what they were saying. CYC would immediately contact the school on my behalf to find out what they said. Then we would either talk on the phone or schedule a time for me to come in to discuss what the conversation was about. The CYC staffs are all very approachable and accessible. Their doors are always open. That's why I feel they are extremely passionate, responsible, and care about us.

Many parents and family members, like Mrs. Wong, viewed HCCC as an extremely vital space for the community.

All of the staff mentioned attending a number of school meetings with parents because "the parents needed someone to be there with them." For instance, Cindy has been to quite a few meetings and open houses with parents since she started in 2002. She stressed that when parents develop a trusting relationship with CYC, they are able to ask the staff members to assist them with institutional matters:

> The parents are very comfortable with us working with their children. And they really know that we are really there to provide any support. ... I would say they feel we are a good resource and provide services. I've been to a few of the school meetings with parents so we help with the translation, provide support, etc. It was a very good experience.

Cindy explained in detail her first time attending school events with parents:

> The first time I went was when I first started working here. I went with the youth and the parent to a parent night at the school. The student was experiencing difficulty in school and the parent didn't know English. The parent asked us if we could go with them because they're recent immigrants. They didn't know anyone in the area who

could help them. I was available and so I went with them to the school. These kinds of contacts are extremely important. Afterwards, the parent was like, "Do you want to join us for dinner?" I was like, "It's okay." They feel really thankful. It was after hours because all the open houses are like 7 or 8 o'clock so they are very appreciative.

In order to contact the school on behalf of the parents, CYC must request and obtain consent from the parents. With the parents' consent, CYC contacts the school on behalf of the parents and family. Cindy explained the process in detail:

When the parents agree, they have to sign a consent form. And then we fax the form to a school [and] directly to that teacher and then we will tell the teacher that we will call you. And after our discussion with the school, we do have a follow-up process. Every month or every other month we would send a letter to the teacher and then in that letter there is a format [that] the teachers can fill out. For instance, is the student meeting all of the expectations? Is the student able to finish up all their homework? How are their testing scores? And what are the grades that they might get? And every time we look at those letters, then we know exactly what's happening. And also we ask the teacher for their syllabus. By this week what should the student learn? So that's how we work with the teacher.

The staff members have had mixed results when contacting the schools and teachers. Cindy found some of the teachers hard to reach, while others were responsive and understanding:

We did have some experience with some teachers who either they lacked the time or I'm not sure what's the reason ... but they are hard to reach. Or when we send them the letter they might say they never received it. But then we do come across a lot of teachers who are really, really caring for the students and who respond to us in just a second.

Other staff also echoed Cindy's sentiment. Erin recalled receiving "a pretty positive response" from two high schools. For example, Erin was welcomed when she gave a talk about CYC's services during a guidance counselor staff meeting at one of the public high schools in Harborview. At the same time, "negative interactions" occurred for the most part at the other high schools. For instance, Erin helped a family write a letter to the student's high school relating to an upcoming Individualized Education Program (IEP) meeting because the parent did not understand English. With the parent's approval, Erin was able to obtain a copy of the student's IEP. After reviewing the file, Erin noted that the school had not been addressing the student's needs. Furthermore, the student's most recent IEP was dated a year and a half earlier, but the document was never signed; and thus, the meeting was not validated.

Additionally, a reevaluation, which must occur at least once every three years, was supposed to be scheduled for that same year, yet there appeared to be no record that it took place. After over a month and several attempts to schedule a meeting, the IEP meeting was confirmed. The day of the meeting, Erin along with HCCC's Family Support Coordinator, who has been working closely with the family, went to the school with the parent. The family support coordinator served as the translator while Erin advocated for the parent and the student. A total of seven people were present at the IEP meeting (three school personnel, Erin, the family support coordinator, the parent, and the student). At the meeting, Erin asked "about accountability, how they communicate or maintain communication with parents, their timeliness on getting thing down, following special ed. rules and laws." She felt the school was "very annoyed" by her questions because, she explained, "I don't think they were really used to being questioned about accountability and special education laws. So I think they were very annoyed with me because I was catching them probably breaking laws." The school personnel's annoyance is an example of the disrespect frequently displayed towards immigrant families of color. Erin shared an incident that occurred at the meeting, which I noted in my field notes:

> Erin asked the school personnel why an annual reevaluation of the student's IEP never took place and that the IEP stated the school would provide the student additional support during the school day, yet nothing occurred. It was during this time that the teachers turned to the parent and told them that their child is lazy because they never completed their assignments. The environment suddenly turned "very tense." The parent started crying and the student as well. With tears coming down their face, the student kept apologizing to their mother, which Erin noted as "especially hard to watch." Rather than working with the parents, student and HCCC, the teachers appeared to be blaming the student when Erin requested clarification from the school.

At the end of the meeting and after Erin pushed for more services and support for the student, the school agreed to offer an extra class period of special education for the student. While glad to have attended the meeting with the family, Erin expressed the blatant inequalities and differences in respect and services that exist in many school districts that serve predominantly low-income and immigrant families. She explained:

> It's just really sad. It's just really sad that there's so much red tape and bureaucracy to get anything done. Whereas, if you're a parent living in a middle-income or a nice environment, you can just say, "hey, this is wrong." and they will fix it. No problem. They will do it for you. But for the Harborview public school system, or any urban district, there's so much red tape. It's just awful.

Noam, Biancarosa, and Dechausay (2003) explain that there are three modes of bridging between schools and afterschool programs: interpersonal, curricular, and systemic. Cindy and Erin's descriptions of their interactions with the schools fall under the "interpersonal" bridging since it "ranges from serendipitous meetings between school and afterschool personnel to regular contact between school and afterschool staff via phone, email, and other means" (Noam et al., 2003, p. 13). According to their research, the interpersonal domain is the most common and the success "depends upon whether the flow of information is reciprocal or one way" (p. 13). Listening to the staffs share their experiences with the different schools, it appears while there are schools where the flow of information is one way, there are others that are reciprocal. Interestingly, similar to Delgado-Gaitan (2004), the schools where the flow of information is more reciprocal are the bilingual elementary and middle schools. The challenges that the CYC staffs noted were the difficulty of establishing and maintaining contact with the schools since schools often do not have a family and community liaison on a regular basis. As a result, the responsibility to bridge the school and family often falls on the out-of-school time programs (Noam et al., 2003). Jeff reflected on a meeting that he attended at one of the high schools because the student was skipping school:

> The student just kept falling through the cracks and nobody at the school cared or saw it … the school never bothered to do anything. I mean if you're a nice kid, they don't notice you and you just keep cracking and cracking and then when you are about to fall that's when someone realizes "Wow, there's a child here." … Now they are labeled as "bad kids". That's how it usually goes.

As a result, CYC advocates for the youth and their families, who as I have shown in previous chapters might not be aware of their rights. Cindy explained:

> Helping the youth is extremely important because teachers might not have enough time to really know and understand a student's background. As a result, teachers sometimes might not be aware of the background of the student. When the youth comes to CYC, we might get to know their other side. We would be able to provide those kinds of information to the teacher and school. For instance, if the student is really quiet and shy at school, it doesn't mean the student has a speech problem or needs to be in ESL. If we know the student, we could provide a different perspective to the school. Our goal is for the school to better obtain more information and understand the student in order to make a better plan for the student.

Jeff and Cindy amplified the dangers of the model minority myth and perpetual foreigner since Asian American students are often viewed as the "nice kids" or "ESL bound."

Parents reflected positively about the services at CYC and the "dedication" of the staff members in advocating for their child(ren) and family. A parent of a middle school youth expressed:

> I really think all of the staffs at CYC treat my son very, very well. They would let me know about anything that is a concern or any news. Cindy would update me about his homework and tutoring sessions. Erin offered to come to one of my son's school meetings. She called to check-in with me one day and I told her I have a meeting with the teachers. Erin said she is available and that she would be able to come with me to the meeting. We went to the meeting together. All of the staffs here are very caring and they really want to help my son. My son really loves coming to CYC. He comes here right after school. He truly loves coming here.

Another parent shared their experiences with CYC and its staffs:

> I truly believe CYC can help the youth. I really feel that the time they put in my child is a lot and even more time than I do. I truly believe the staff members have a lot of responsibility and they do really help the young people. They want to help as well. You can say the staff members have helped the youth or you can say they have helped the parents. In a sense, the staffs are really a bridge because they are able to communicate with multiple sides, the parents, child, and school.

Even after the staffs have left CYC, many of the parents still maintain contact with them, particularly the parents with children that have been coming for several years. Parents would ask current and former staffs advice and feedbacks regarding their child(ren). For instance, it was early June and Mrs. Wong was worried since none of Joe's college letters still have arrived. She contacted one of the former staff, Peter, for assistance since he had worked closely with the family:

> Colleges were starting soon but his acceptance and financial aid packages haven't arrived yet ... I was extremely worried so I called Peter for some assistance. I said 'Joe still doesn't know which college he is going in the fall. What should we do?' Peter said he'll schedule a time to meet with Joe and they'll go to the colleges to check on his status. One afternoon, Peter took Joe to all of the schools. Later that day, Peter called and told me what happened at each of the schools. Peter is an extremely dedicated person and has helped us tremendously over the years.

In other words, through developing *and* maintaining a trusting relationship with the CYC staff, parents and youth felt comfortable asking for CYC's assistance. Mrs. Wong highlights how the CYC staffs continuously go above and beyond in advocating and supporting her family. She explains:

> I truly believe CYC helps the youth ... they put in a lot of time and energy in my child and sometimes even more time than I am able to do. I truly believe the staffs are very

responsible and caring. They really help the youth. You can say the staff have helped the youth or you can say they have helped the parents … they are able to communicate with and understand both sides—the parents and the child. I will always be grateful for what they have done for my family.

Moreover, CYC and HCCC acknowledge the cultural wealth of the families that they serve. As a result, they are a part of the community where people find their services and programs to be relevant.

Conclusion

As I have illustrated in this chapter, children of immigrants from low-income and working-class backgrounds experience difficulty in negotiating the many different expectations placed on them. By finding additional resources such as attending and building their own networks of support through ethnic CBOs, like CYC, the youth are able to bridge their "multiple worlds." Additionally, parents and families also view such services valuable for them. Essentially, HCCC and CYC play a dual role in helping low-income and working-class immigrant families achieve the dominant culture's social capital while maintaining and appreciating their own cultural wealth. HCCC has developed and maintained a trusting relationship in the community and understands how to access the dominant discourse. Therefore, "CYC is like a bridge to society," expressed Peter. "This bridge could expand to the schools, the parents, and community." In the following chapter, I will discuss CYC's role in creating and maintaining a sense of youth (comm) unity for Chinese American young people from low-income and working-class immigrant families.

Note

1. During February vacation, I facilitated a workshop series on Angel Island, a detention center where mostly Chinese and Asian immigrants were detained for days to years at a time from 1910 to 1940.

Works cited

Christensen, L. (2009). Putting out the linguistic welcome mat. In W. Au (Ed.), *Rethinking multicultural education* (pp. 89–96). Milwaukee, WI: Rethinking Schools.

Delgado-Gaitan, C. (2004). *Involving Latino families in schools: Raising student achievement through home-school partnerships*. Thousand Oaks, CA: Corwin Press.

Delpit, L. (1988). The silenced dialogue: Power and pedagogy in educating other people's children. *Harvard Educational Review, 58*(3), 280–298.

Delpit, L. (1995). *Other people's children: Cultural conflict in the classroom*. New York, NY: The New Press.

Delpit, L. (2009). Ebonics and culturally responsive instruction. In W. Au (Ed.), *Rethinking multicultural education* (pp. 121–130). Milwaukee, WI: Rethinking Schools.

Gibson, M. A. (1988). *Accommodation without assimilation: Sikh immigrants in an American high school*. Ithaca, NY: Cornell University Press.

Kwak, K. (2003, March–June). Adolescents and their parents: A review of intergenerational family relations for immigrant and non-immigrant families. *Journal of Human Development, 46*, 115–136.

Lee, S. J. (2005). *Up against Whiteness: Race, school and immigrant youth*. New York, NY: Teachers College Press.

Lew, J. (2003). The (re)construction of second-generation ethnic networks: Structuring academic success of Korean American high school students. In C. C. Park, A. L. Goodwin, & S. J. Lee (Eds.), *Asian American identities, families, and schooling* (pp. 157–176). Greenwich, CT: Information Age Publishing.

Louie, V. S. (2004). *Compelled to excel: Immigration, education, and opportunity among Chinese Americans*. Stanford, CA: Stanford University Press.

Noam, G. G., Biancarosa, G., & Dechausay, N. (2003). *Afterschool education: Approaches to an emerging field*. Cambridge, MA: Harvard Education Press.

Phelan, P., Davidson, A. L., & Yu, H. C. (1991). Students' multiple worlds: Negotiating the boundaries of family, peer, and school cultures. *Anthropology & Education Quarterly, 22*(3), 224–250.

Phelan, P., Davidson, A. L., & Yu, H. C. (1993). Students' multiple worlds: Navigating the borders of family, peer, and the school cultures. In P. Phelan & A. L. Davidson (Eds.), *Renegotiating cultural diversity in American school* (pp. 52–88). New York, NY: Teachers College Press.

Phelan, P., Davidson, A. L., & Yu, H. C. (1998). *Adolescents' worlds: Negotiating family, peers, and school*. New York, NY: Teachers College Press.

Portes, A., & Rumbaut, R. G. (2001). *Legacies: The story of the immigrant second generation*. Berkeley, CA: University of California Press.

Qin, D. B. (2006). "Our child doesn't talk to us anymore": Alienation in immigrant Chinese families. *Anthropology & Educational Quarterly, 37*(2), 162–179.

Suárez-Orozco, C., & Suárez-Orozco, M. M. (2001). *Children of immigration*. Cambridge, MA: Harvard University Press.

Sung, B. L. (1987). *The adjustment experiences of Chinese immigrant children in New York City*. New York, NY: Center for Migration Studies.

Valdés, G. (1996). *Con respecto: Bridging the distances between culturally diverse families and schools*. New York, NY: Teachers College Press.

Wong, N. W. A. (2008). "They see us as resource": The role of a community-based youth center in supporting the academic lives of low-income Chinese American Youth. *Anthropology & Education Quarterly, 39*(2), 181–204.

Wong, N. W. A. (2013). "Like a bridge": How a community-based organization helps immigrant and working poor Chinese parents navigate U.S. schools. In R. Endo & X. L. Rong (Eds.), *Educating Asian Americans: Achievement, schooling, and identities* (pp. 181–204). Charlotte, NC: Information Age Publishing.

CHAPTER SIX

The importance of youth (comm)unity

CYC is a home for me. We are buddies here. Home is not only family. Home is a place where people can learn from each other and you can be yourself. You feel warm and accepted. You can learn and share with others. Home is a place where you can learn, you feel warm, you can share with each other and you have confidence. Everybody is happy. We play ping-pong and people would say, "Let's play." Or in band, we are willing to help each other. Everyone here is helping each other to have a positive relationship. Not a lot of places can do that. It's not easy to make young people want to talk a lot. It's sometimes very difficult. Young people have different ways of talking and it's hard to understand; but here, you can see the youth and the staffs can talk very well.

—KEVIN, SEVENTEEN YEAR OLD YOUTH

I had known Kevin for two years when we sat down for our first interview in 2007. When we first met, he had immigrated to the United States a year ago with his parents and younger sister and described himself as a "very shy" high school fresh-man. Similar to the majority of the youth, Kevin heard about CYC through his friends—ethnic networks (Louie, 2004; Zhou & Bankston, 1998). While learn-ing English and enrolling in other academic programs was what brought him to CYC, Kevin began participating in other CYC programs. Previously, Kevin had participated in other out-of-school programs, but he explained that CYC was "more dynamic" due to the wide range of programs available and the relationships he established with the staffs and other youth. "After I started coming to CYC," explained Kevin, "my mom noticed a change in me, that I am more social and involved in the community. She was happy for me."

Cindy, CYC Tutoring Coordinator, explains the importance of building and maintaining a "good relationship" with the youth as a key factor for the CYC staffs.

> A lot of the youth have really good relationship with the staffs. So they know we're open door. We are a place for them to hang out and to chat. If they want to say something, there are people who are here and who would listen to them.

Yohalem (2003) points out that "[r]espect and trust are critical ingredients of meaningful relationships between youth and adults" (p. 361). Besides respect and trust, she also mentions time as a critical ingredient. Yohalem explains, "[t]ime spent informally 'hanging out' with youth and time spent participating in shared experiences is what creates … positive youth-adult interactions and a sense of community" (p. 362). As Calderón (1998) argues, "Without a sense of belonging to the mainstream culture, the student can either withdraw or become part of a group that does accept her or him. All too often, these groups are gangs" (p. 70). Piha and Adams (2001), in the Community Network for Youth Development (CNYD), adds if youth are unable to obtain and access positive supports and opportunities, "we may see them seeking these experiences in troubling ways: looking for challenge in ways that put them at risk, belonging to gangs, or seeking safety through violence" (p. 22).

Cindy explained the process of building trust with young people requires time and understanding: "It takes time and it also depends on the youth. I won't say just for an instant … if you step in here we're going to be really friendly … it takes time." Some of the youth need more time to "open up" and so we would take a longer time to open up. Additionally, trust is another crucial element. Through developing trust with the CYC staffs, the young people view CYC as a resource and support. Cindy noted CYC's approach in establishing and maintaining relationships with the young people:

> All of the youth come and they stay here. If the students have any problems or issues, they would come up to a staff because they trusted the staff. We try to help them and we're good listeners … So that's how in the long run, they start building a sense of security and they start developing relationship with us. It's a very long process. Over the years, it's just checking in with them. That's how we started it. For example, when they come in just say, "Hi, how are you? How's your day?" And if they have any questions or anything we are always there. If you consistently do that, of course you're gonna be able to develop trust.

By emphasizing an ongoing process of regularly checking in with the youth and understanding that time and trust are critical, authentic, and meaningful relationships are formed at CYC. Moreover, each of the staff members works one-on-one with the youth—depending on who the youth is able to develop a closer relationship with. Peter, a former Youth Worker at CYC, mentioned, "... if we can't build that trust with them then we won't be able to communicate in any way." CYC serves as a bridge because they understand the majority of the youths' parents are limited in English and work long hours.

As youth and community workers, the CYC staffs acknowledge the various requirements that the profession entails and strives to maintain the balance of direct interactions with the young people and their families and the behind-the-scenes work (e.g., paperwork, meeting with funders, lesson planning, etc.). When Wai-Ming was the director of CYC, she explained the importance of balancing the administrative work with the one-on-one interactions. Grant writing, preparing reports, and meeting with board members, (potential) funders and government elected officials according Wai-Ming, are important, but interacting and maintaining relationships with youth is just as important:

> At least one day or two days I need to be on the floor and interacting with the youth. So I have three days to focus on the administrative matters and that's it. But if it's time for reporting then I need to focus more on the administrative side. Basically, my 5 days work week is 3 days in the office and 2 days on the floor. I need to maintain that relationship with the youth to build the program, otherwise I don't know their needs and there will be no program. You know, I started off as a direct staff, too. I like spending time with the youth. So it's about balancing. It's really knowing my limits and setting a structure for myself.

For the youth in this research, CYC provides a sense of "belonging" (Calderón, 1998), "positive support" (Piha & Adams, 2001), trust and love. In other words, CYC offers "authentic caring" for young people (Valenzuela, 1999). At CYC, the staff members have the *time* to develop reciprocity and have the *cultural understanding* of both worlds, whereas at home, their parents/families long work hours and might not always understand the dominant culture and at school, their teachers and administrators "just don't care." Therefore, CYC is a place *and* space where young people are able to find a sense of community that they feel trusted and loved, which I will show in greater detail below.

"Cuz they care about those who goes there": Providing a sense of family

Several of the young people began to increasingly attend CYC after participating in some of the programs. For instance, during the after school hours, since both of their parents work long hours and "there's no one at home," Calvin and Jerry, who were both in sixth grade, started coming to CYC regularly. They, in particular, "enjoy the games" at CYC (e.g., Game Cube and computer games). Also, since the majority of the youth live in public housing in Harborview or small apartments in Chinatown, their living space is tightly confined, and thus oftentimes would be a challenge to find enough space to study and relax.

Additionally, parents have expressed their appreciation of CYC's services and support. Mrs. Mui shares the significant relationship that CYC have for youth and their families. In particular, she explains due to their long and inflexible work hours, Mr. and Mrs. Mui are unable to be home after school.

> There are some households that have a small family, and so coming to CYC is like a large family here. You are able to communicate and share things with the staffs and the other youth about school, life, and different things. As a result, you are learning many things. If you are an only child then you often are all alone. Coming home from school, they would do their homework by themselves, because the parents work long hours as well as have limited English. Then when the parents come home, since we speak Cantonese, we are unable to help with their homework. What we see and know is limited. However, CYC is different. There are different age groups and people go to different schools here. As a result, they are able to learn from each other and under-stand things more. That's why CYC is a really good place for the youth.

As I examined in Chapter 3, parents expressed the triangulated tension they expe-rienced due to their long and inflexible work hours, limited understanding of the U.S. education system, and the schools' lack of multilingual and multicultural ser-vices are obstacles for them to feel welcome in their children's schools. As a result, many parents view themselves as unable to help their children anymore. "What we see and know is limited," as expressed by Mrs. Mui.

The youth also appreciate CYC as a "comfortable" and "welcoming" place and space. For instance, Steven said, "We all get along here and the staff members are nice and don't yell at people" and "they are a lot funnier and they joke with us more." Teachers, on the other hand, "don't understand us." Many of the youth were comfortable when they first started coming to CYC, because "the people who work here made me feel comfortable." Sarah explained, "The staffs are nice. They talk to you, but they won't get in your business or if you don't wanna talk about something they just don't push you. Not like the teachers, they don't care about us." Yun-Yun, a ninth grader who immigrated to the United States in 2003 with her parents and younger brother, started coming to CYC shortly after she came to the United States. Yun-Yun said the reason she continues to come to CYC is because "I've built a close relationship with everyone here—the staffs and the other youth. I met a lot of my friends at CYC and we are still friends today." Other youth also noted similar statements:

It's just a place where I really want to go every day. I look forward to coming to CYC.
—JERRY, 6TH GRADER

CYC is actually a place where I became more open and I made a lot of new friends here ... I met all of them here. I like it here and I volunteer here a lot more than any other place cuz I've been here since 7th grade. It's a second home. I hang out here a lot. It's the people here like the staffs. I actually like it.
—SARAH, 10TH GRADER

You are at home with family when you are CYC. A family makes someone feel a sense of happiness, joy, and at peace. When the staffs or other people help us, we would be extremely thankful and appreciative. You learn that you are not alone in this world; rather there are people who care about you, understand you, take care of you, and look out for you. I don't need to worry about life when I come to CYC. If someone is able to find happiness in their life, then they feel hopeful and have goals and aspirations in life. Once you have goals, you have the motivation to push yourself in reaching for those goals. That's how I feel about CYC.
—BECKY, 8TH GRADER

Unlike school where "authentic caring" seemed to be limited or a shortcoming for many of the youth, CYC, on the other hand, is able to provide such space for them.

Additionally, while a number of the youth have been to other OST programs they prefer CYC to the others. For example, a few of the youth attended other OST programs that solely focused on academic tutoring and test preparation classes, but they did not feel "connected" or a sense of "caring" was not present for them. One of the youth reflected on his experience at another OST program: "I don't feel comfortable at that place. Not like the way I do at CYC. The staffs there didn't connect with us like the CYC staff. You know, the CYC staffs always check in and cared about us." Wendy, a graduating high school senior, reflected on her experiences at CYC to an out-of-school program that she attended when she was younger:

I went to this afterschool program when I was in elementary school, but I don't remember feeling like I was a part a family. I mean like I knew some of the staffs. I remember going up to them. Sometimes they be giving me cookies or something and patting me on the head and be like "go play" or something. [laughs] But I didn't feel this family thing going on at all, like big sister and little sister or brother relationships at CYC. It was just like they're there to help but that's it. I'm just happy for the younger teens at CYC, because the staffs care.

When I asked Wendy how she defines caring, her response was someone who is considerate and culturally understanding:

I wouldn't say pay attention to the person a lot. I mean it's just pretty natural. If someone was alone than the CYC staffs or older teens would go up to him or her and just start talking and be like, "Oh, do you want to play a game or something?" and start chatting, "How's your day at school?" or "What are you going to do tomorrow?" something like, just like chat with them. And if they're happy or anything just be happy with them. They just take notice of you, basically. That's what all the kids want, right. Just get notice. If you're in trouble, people at CYC see it and then they start talking to you and then they actually help you.

Interestingly, Wendy compared CYC to Big Brothers Big Sisters, one of the largest youth mentoring organizations in the United States, but "without having to say it" in their name:

Cuz like when I see the older teens, *we* all look after the younger teens. We don't stare at them 24/7 and watch after every movement, but we notice what they're doing. And like if something is weird than we just take notice of it and we ask them. And then you hangout not just like friends, but just like brothers and sisters ... For example, if I walk into CYC right now, that's what I would see. It feels nice ... just to have somewhere you can turn to and chat, just about anything.

Tina, also a graduating high school senior, expressed how she views CYC as family: "It's more free here ... CYC is more like a family. You really feel close to the people like a family so that's nice." Piha and Adams (2001) note:

[w]hen young people feel respected and have caring relationships with adults and peers in an after-school program, they feel more included and invested in the program. As they develop a sense of group membership, they are more likely to attend regularly and participate more fully in the program. (p. 59)

The young people held a deep sense of trust and respect for CYC and saw each other as a family. Similarly, in Thai's study (2002) of young adult second generation Vietnamese Americans, he states that "... the ideology of family collectivism is also practiced in the realm of friendship and, as such, friends are often spoken of as family" (p. 56). CYC illustrates a clear example of collectivism among ethnic peer groups. In being with their "sisters" and/or "brothers," the youth are with family who support, respect, and encourage them when the dominant society is unable to do so and their immigrant parents have limited "dominant cultural capital" (Carter, 2005). Therefore, being associated with "brotherhood" and "sisterhood" means family, friendship, and community.

In addition to having a reciprocal "authentic caring" relationship (Valenzuela, 1999) with their peers at CYC, the young people are also developing such a relationship with the staff members (i.e., multireciprocal relationships). I recalled in my field notes when Peter, a former CYC Youth Worker, visited CYC, all of the youth ecstatically greeted him:

> Peter came out to the main area from the staffs' office at around 2:55 p.m. Today was the first time I saw Peter since I've been back, which has been close to two years. He was smiling as he came out and said hi to both Erin and myself. All the youth immediately said: "Hi, Peter!" Some of the youth even screamed out his name or joyfully repeated his name more than once. There was a clear sense of respect and friendship between Peter and the youth (Field notes, January 5, 2007).

As I have shown, the youth are able to develop a trusting relationship with the staff members at CYC. In general, CYC is a space where the youth are welcomed and respected.

Additionally, CYC alumni, who are in their early 20s, would often visit and volunteer at CYC and thus there is a sense of appreciation and respect for CYC. For instance, "the youth who are now in their 20s, I mean some of them still come just to check in with us and things like that," Jeff expressed. "So overall it was positive, you know, for them to have this space." Likewise Peter explained, "There are youth who graduate from college and get a good job so they appreciate us and come back to visit and help out because they know it was hard for them as well." I, too, noticed a lot of the "alums" would visit CYC and some would volunteer their time. For instance, the older youth and alums were all present at the CYC performance where they held a special sendoff show for Peter when he left CYC. In other words, the youth return after they have graduated because CYC, as Yohalem (2003) writes, was able to "create positive [and] safe learning environments."

In addition to trust being established and maintained between the youth and staff members, CYC is a trusted space. For instance, lying openly are a mini snack counter and small refrigerator packed with water, juices, and sodas for people to purchase and a cash box filled with money. The young people understand the importance of trust and thus do not take or steal the food, drinks, and/or cash from CYC. Additionally, they do not take or steal other people's personal belongings. At the same time, individuals who are new at CYC might not have established that sense of trust. For example, one afternoon in early February a youth came in to CYC asking if anyone saw their iPod mini. The youth, who has been coming to CYC on a regular basis, realized it was missing when they got home. A staff member, who started at CYC for a few months replied, "People would take it when things are left around." "People wouldn't steal things. They probably took it by mistake," explained the youth. Another staff added, "They wouldn't take the iPod mini because money is always left lying around at CYC and people don't take it." The next day, we learned one of staff stored the iPod mini inside their desk when the youth left it. In other words, the sense of trust being established and maintained was clearly different for the individuals. While the young person and the staff who did not consider the fact that others had taken the iPod mini, individuals new to CYC often did. A deep sense of trust is present at CYC and everyone understands and respects CYC and one another (i.e., individual as well as group trusts are established at CYC).

Since all of the staff members are also children of immigrants and the majority attended the public schools in the United States, they shared similar experiences that the youth and their families face. Thus, in forming a trusted space, CYC is able to serve as a "second-generation ethnic network" (Lew, 2003) and bridge the youths' "multiple worlds" (Phelan, Davidson, & Yu, 1998). By understanding the youth, parents, and schools, CYC is able to create a sense of trust and care when serving the community. While maintaining the trust, love, and caring that exists at CYC is a collective process of both youth and staff members, it is the staff members who have taken the initiative to promote such environment. Piha and Adams (2001) indicate that one could tell if a program has placed an emphasis on promoting a sense of safety "because the environment is clearly a place where all are included and respected" (p. 33). Piha and Adams also listed several points that a program should have when they are promoting a sense of safety, such as the youth and staff members speak respectfully to each other even when disagreeing, they interact comfortably with one another, and the center's ground rules and schedules are posted, so that the youth and parents can read them. All of Piha and Adams' points were present during the years I was at CYC.

"I want to give back": The Youth Leadership program

CYC offers three leadership programs for middle and high school youth. One of the programs, Youth Leadership, works with fifteen to twenty high school youth. The aim of the year-long leadership and mentorship program is to gain knowledge and awareness about leadership skills and issues in the community. Each of the three to four teams has five to six youth and a staff, whose role is to serve as a facilitator and mentor.

The young people are selected through an interview process where the staff members pose various questions and scenarios. The Youth Leadership members develop workshops and activities and create a newsletter for their peers and serve as mentors for the middle school age youth at CYC. Ming, who was a graduating high school senior and his first year in the program, described the Youth Leadership as "a program that gives youth the opportunity to learn about leadership skills and educate younger youth about different topics through workshops and research."

When I asked some of the Youth Leadership members why they are interested in being a part of Youth Leadership, statements such as "I wanted to learn about and use leadership roles because I never had the opportunity before" and "I want to give back" to CYC and the community were common responses. The Youth Leadership members are required to commit at least 2 hours each week for the team's meetings, in addition to other events such as retreats. A lot of the youth expressed the importance of the retreats, because "all of the teams come together," explained Ming, "and so we got to grow as a group. If we didn't have the retreats then we wouldn't know one another and we wouldn't have the goals for the year." The weekly team meeting is where each team brainstorms, creates, and finalizes their workshops, which is decided among the team members. Tommy explained how the topics are set:

> As a team we would come up with a topic idea based on the team's focus, like health, youth, and community issues. In the beginning, we would figure out what our team topic would be. Everyone would throw out a lot of different ideas. Then we would narrow it down by voting on it. That's how we decide on the topic. Once we figure out a topic, the team members would research it. During the research process, we would update our team members on what we have found. Then when we are done research-ing, we would decide what we should present about that particular topic. We learn how to create effective PowerPoint slides, which is good to know.

One of the workshop topics was bullying. As mentioned in Chapter 4, since several of the young people experienced hostility, exclusion, and bullying in school, they want to open the dialogue for middle school youth to discuss ways in approaching the issue. Yee-Mun explained:

> Being Asian living in the U.S., we would experience discrimination in our lives and so we want to teach the middle school teens not to bully others or what to do when they encounter bullying. In middle school, bullying occurs because people feel they have more power when they bully others. We also talked about if other people bully them, what they should do, because they are still young and might not know how to address the issue and protect themselves.

Albert, a former Youth Leadership member and now in his first year in college, stated the importance of the workshops, particularly the youth-led component:

> The workshops are good because it teach the youth stuff that they don't know. With workshops, not every program has workshops for kids that are run by their peers or older teens. We do a lot more workshops than other places. It's helpful to learn about different things like public speaking, research, teamwork, and using PowerPoint. Besides, when high school students are doing the workshops, it can be more effective because the middle school students look up to them.

Each team has a team leader that is voted among the individual team members. For instance, one year Tommy was a team leader in the youth issues team. Instead of running meetings on his own, Tommy encouraged all of his team members to facilitate meetings and discussions. He explained:

> We would take turn facilitating the meetings because we want to provide more opportunity for everyone to speak up and contribute in the group. We don't want people to sit around and not say anything. Each of the group is not that big and so it's easier to connect with your team members. Once you're able to build relationships then everyone would be able to feel really comfortable in voicing their thoughts and opinions.

Additionally, at the end of the year, all of the teams would come together as a collective in creating and developing a community event. One year, members of all three teams decided to focus on the Chinatown library project because according to Philip, who was a Youth Leadership member that year, "we were all shocked that there is no library in Chinatown, especially since there was one fifty years ago." Jeff expressed how a library creates vibrant resources for a community and brings people together. At the same time, he explained why there is a constant struggle for working poor communities, such as Harborview's Chinatown, to achieve such goal:

> Chinatown doesn't have a library. Libraries are usually places where grandparents take the kids cuz there's story times. It goes back to this thing why the working poor are not involved in school. It's usually a place grandparent or parents take their children to do research, for college info and financial aid, for storytelling. It kind of shows that the affluent have certain resources that working people or working poor people don't have. All of Harborview's communities have libraries. However, Chinatown does not have it. Almost all of the major Chinatowns in the U.S. have a library. So for a progressive city like Harborview, the working poor just have very little resources to work with.

After learning more about the Chinatown library project, the Youth Leadership members decided to create a petition to bring back a public library to Chinatown. Since the majority of the youth were bilingual, they were able to divide up into multilingual teams (e.g., Cantonese, Mandarin, and English). The teams went to different areas in Chinatown such as the YMCA, Hope Elementary School, Asian supermarkets, and daycare centers. Some of the youth went to Hope Elementary School after school was dismissed and outreached to parents and families. In the end, they were able to obtain several hundred signatures. They brought the petition to the city mayor's attention because "we want to convince the mayor to open up a library in Chinatown." Both the youth and the Youth Leadership staff attended the city council meeting when the Chinatown library branch issue was scheduled on the agenda. According to Jeff, "There were actually a lot of young people from the community that turned out." However, only two out of the seven city council members were present at the meeting and thus the issue was placed on hold. To this day, the Chinatown library branch is still on hold. After attending the city council meeting, a number of the youth were outraged by the absences of the City Council members. Jeff said:

> It shows how little that this community really matters and the youth saw that. They know what happened. So yeah, the youth were asking 'how come, you know, these two people are making the decision for all of us.' I told them, 'you know that's why you we need to read the newspapers, attend community meetings, and understand who is representing you.' I mean these are really important. It just shows how little, you know, this community really, really matters to the city.

While the library project is still on hold, CYC provided a culturally relevant (Ladson-Billings, 1994) space for young people to "develop a critical consciousness" of what is happening in their community and "challenging the status quo of the current social order."

Youth Leadership members have repeatedly expressed the benefits of the Youth Leadership program. For instance, one of the youth said, "I've learned a lot from joining the Youth Leadership program. It's a really good program." I asked Mun-Yee, a sophomore in high school and a first year Youth Leadership member, to explain what Youth Leadership means to her:

> We learn about leadership skills. We learn how to collaborate with our peers. I also learned listening skills, like we need to listen when others are talking and not interrupt them or say something that is irrelevant. Also, there are times where people would disagree with you and so you need to learn how to handle yourself in those situations.

Here are some of the responses from youth about the benefits of joining the Youth Leadership program:

> I do feel the Youth Leadership program has helped me. I am a part of my school's Asian Club and from the leadership skills that I learned from being a part of Youth Leadership, I am able to use those skills in the Asian Club, such as leading discussions and public speaking. During the Lunar New Year celebration, we organized an event at school. We made food and had a karaoke contest that day.
> —YEE, 10TH GRADER AND FIRST YEAR IN YOUTH LEADERSHIP

> I learned communication and leadership skills. I definitely met new friends.
> —TINA, GRADUATING SENIOR AND FIRST YEAR IN YOUTH LEADERSHIP

I've gained leadership skills from being a part of Youth Leadership. I learned to be patient when working as a team. The Youth Leadership program has helped me a lot. It's good because it teaches you how to do an interview or how to create a PowerPoint presentation. These skills are useful later on. I think these are useful and good skills to know. I wouldn't have learned it if I wasn't in the program.

—STEVEN, 11TH GRADER AND PAST YOUTH LEADERSHIP MEMBERS

CYC's youth leadership program offers young people opportunities to "solve the problems of his or her physical and social environment" (Boggs, 1971).

"Asian Pride": Providing a sense of ethnic self and identity

Since most of the young people tend to perceive a lack of an "authentic caring" (Valenzuela, 1999) in the schools and since they view schools as a space of "subtractive schooling" (Valenzuela, 1999), they consider themselves as residing in the margins of the school community (Lee, 2005; Olsen, 1997). On the other hand, the young people feel CYC provides them with a space where they could feel a sense of their ethnic self and identity. The youth were able to comfortably speak Cantonese at CYC, but not at school because "people make fun of us [for speaking Cantonese]." In doing so, CYC acknowledges the youths' home culture by "develop[ing] and maintain[ing] [their] cultural competence," which is one of the points of culturally relevant pedagogy (Ladson-Billings, 1995, p. 160). For instance, I recall on several occasions that the youth would yell out "Asian Pride," talk about various topics related to Asian American culture (e.g., C-pop, J-pop and K-pop,[1] manga,[2] popular drama series from Asia, etc.), sing karaoke or feel comfortable bringing and eating Chinese and other Asian food at CYC. A number of the youth would wait until after school to eat lunch because "the school lunches are nasty and expensive" and "people would look at you weird for bringing food from home." In other words, Asian Americans often experience "lunch box moments" during their K-12 U.S. schooling. Instead, the young people would usually get some pastries, dim sum, dry snacks, or a noodle or rice dish from Chinatown and then eat at CYC.

CYC is able to provide young people a space where they feel welcomed, and in doing so they feel proud of being Chinese American and Asian American while their school settings are not accepting of them. As Reyes (1995) puts it, "For as marginalized individuals ... we understand how we can be here in this place, but not here in this space" (p. 253). In other words, one could be physically present in a place but, at the same time, not be accepted in the space. The young people see their schools as a place that does not acknowledge and respect their culture and heritage and essentially, they feel like they need to "hide" their identities and thus are silenced. Schools for many of the young people become a place that takes their cultural heritage away in order to conform and assimilate to the dominant culture. Since CYC is able to provide them with not just a place, but *also* a space where they could express their "Asian Pride," the young people in this research are free from the dominant White (upper) middle-class hegemonic culture. For instance, a youth reflected, "I thought CYC is cool cuz it is full of Asians and everyone all understand each other, not like school where the teachers and staff just ignore you and think you're lesser then them." In other words, this young person indicated that because schools do not appreciate and understand their Chinese American culture and identity, they feel CYC is able to provide them a sense of ethnic self and identity. Since schools are not settings that accept the youths' identities, CYC is a space where they are able to feel a sense of ethnic understanding and pride, and thus serves as a culturally relevant (Ladson-Billings, 1994) space.

"All they see is the pressure": Providing a sense of being a teenager

As research has shown, in a lot of low-income and working-class immigrant families, role reversal between immigrant parents and their children is extremely common where the children assist their parents in a new society (Kibria, 1993; Lee, 2005; Lee & Kumashiro, 2005; Suárez-Orozco & Suárez-Orozco, 2001; Sung, 1987). Sung (1987) writes, "Instead of the child looking to his [or her or their] parents for guidance, support and leadership, the roles are reversed" (p. 166). In other words, immigrant parents from working-class backgrounds are now depending on their children to help them negotiate and navigate with the outside world (i.e., the United States) because their children "typically come into contact with American culture sooner" than they do (Suárez-Orozco & Suárez-Orozco, 2001, p. 73). Furthermore, as I have shown in the previous chapters, since a lot of the youth at CYC have parents who work long hours in restaurants and factory jobs they either have to take care of themselves during the after school to late in the evening hours or in addition have to take care of their siblings.

As I have illustrated throughout this book, a lot of the youth have added responsibilities because their parents are low-income immigrants who do not understand the U.S. American system and are in a culture that has labeled them as deficient. The experiences of the young people are similar to those of children of immigrants in other research who have to help their parents negotiate life in the

United States (Kibria, 1993; Lee & Kumashiro, 2005; Suárez-Orozco & Suárez-Orozco, 2001; Waters, 1999). Children of immigrants might have to translate various forms, go with their elders to different institutions, take care of their younger siblings, contribute to the family income, or help out with the household chores in addition to focusing on academics. Huifen remembered learning how to write a check at CYC, which she credited as important and memorable:

> One thing I remembered the most, the staff taught us how to write a check. It was interesting because I didn't know how. After that, I actually helped my mom write a check. I felt they teach us very practical stuff, not just stuff you learn in school, but the day-to-day basis, too. Learning how to write checks was very memorable to me.

I recall several conversations with Wai-Ming in which she mentioned to me that once CYC closes, a lot of the young people, both the younger and older youth, head back to an empty home and have to cook their own dinners. One of the middle school youth noted to me that his specialty dish is eggs and beef and he would cook dinner four times a week while his parents are at work. Several of the young people shared with me stories of having to buy take-outs at local restaurants in Chinatown or McDonald's because their parents do not return home past 11 p.m. Usually they are the ones who stay until CYC closes. As a result, "they are learning things that most American kids don't even know until they get to college and some of them even later," remarked Jeff. "All they see is the pressure. And the negative is, you know, in terms of growing up as a teenager, you have to grow a lot faster." Freire (1996) similarly writes about his childhood in Brazil, "We were children prematurely forced to become adults. Our childhood was squeezed out between toys and work, between freedom and need" (p. 19).

I first met Michelle, a sixth grader at the time, in 2005. Like a number of the other young people in this research she has added responsibilities at home. Michelle always needed to help her mother fill out governmental housing forms, health forms, and job application forms. Additionally, Michelle holds various responsibilities in her family. For instance, she would pick her little brother up from the afterschool program and would watch her brother during vacation. This gave Michelle added responsibility, especially being a teenager.

Similarly, Po-Yee helps her parents out whenever possible by doing different household chores such as washing the dishes, the laundry, mopping the floors, go grocery shopping with her mother, and cooking dinner. She would also help fill out forms and translate letters for her parents. However, if she does not understand something she will bring the letter and/or forms to CYC and ask the staff for assistance. Po-Yee explained, "I could ask them about any questions that I might have. And sometimes, I would bring them the letters that I don't understand and ask them to help me with it." For instance, because she was not accepted to an exam school, Po-Yee had to decide which traditional public high school would be good for her to attend. I remember one day at CYC, she was asking Wai-Ming about the different high schools because Po-Yee's parents are unable to assist her through this process. Wai-Ming then showed her the school district's website and then guided her through the various links on the site. I also tried to help answer some of the questions that she had regarding the different schools. Therefore, through the assistance of CYC, the young people are able to have a better understanding of the wide range of institutional forms and applications.

Children of low-income immigrants, in other words, are forced to grow up sooner than their middle-class peers. They serve as translators for their elders, babysitters, or second mothers/fathers to their younger siblings when their parents work long hours, bill payers for the household, and additional income earners to their family, unlike their classmates who are able to keep the money for their personal usage. As a result, these young people are unable to participate in extra-curricular activities or hang out with their friends and are also carrying a lot of weight at a very young age. Therefore, CYC is a place where they could *be* teen-agers and have a sense of community even though it might be just for 3–5 hours in a day before returning to an empty house and/or taking care of the household. Many of the youth, like Wayne, a graduating high school senior, view CYC as "a place to de-stress" themselves. In doing so, CYC serves as a youth (comm)unity by providing a welcoming and supportive space between the youths' "multiple worlds" (Phelan et al., 1998).

Conclusion

This chapter illustrated the important role of CBOs that serve low-income and working-class children of immigrants and their families. Specifically, as I have shown, CYC is able to provide low-income Chinese American middle and high school-age youth in Harborview a sense of youth (comm)unity space—a space that is outside of the home and school and consists of bridging the "multiple worlds," multireciprocal "authentic caring," and "culturally relevant" under-standing. Moreover, I have tried to show how CYC's programs, activities, and other approaches all reflect back to their mission statement: to assist the youth in building their academic, social, emotional, and leadership skills by working with the youth, their family, and school. CYC reminds everyone the importance of youth (comm)unity and that a holistic approach is necessary when serving the community.

Notes

1. C-pop means Chinese popular music, J-pop means Japanese popular music, and K-pop means Korean popular music.
2. Manga means comics in Japanese.

Works cited

Boggs, G. L. (1971). *Education to govern* [Pamphlet]. Detroit, MI: All-African People's Union.

Calderón, M. (1998). Adolescent sons and daughters of immigrants: How schools can respond. In K. Borman & B. Schneider (Eds.), *The adolescent years: Social influences and educational challenges* (pp. 65–87). Chicago, IL: The National Society for the Study of Education.

Carter, P. L. (2005). *Keepin' it real: School success beyond black and white*. New York, NY: Oxford University Press.

Freire, P. (1996). *Letters to Cristina: Reflections of my life and work*. New York, NY: Routledge.

Kibria, N. (1993). *Family tightrope: The changing lives of Vietnamese Americans*. Princeton, NJ: Princeton University Press.

Ladson-Billings, G. (1994). *Dreamkeepers: Successful teachers of African American children*. San Francisco, CA: Jossey-Bass.

Ladson-Billings, G. (1995). But that's just good teaching! The case for culturally relevant pedagogy. *Theory Into Practice, 34*(3), 159–165.

Lee, S. J. (2005). *Up against Whiteness: Race, school and immigrant youth*. New York, NY: Teachers College Press.

Lee, S. J., & Kumashiro, K. K. (2005). *NEA's A report on the status of Asian Americans and Pacific Islanders in education: Beyond the "model minority" stereotype*. Washington, DC: National Education Association.

Lew, J. (2003). The (re)construction of second-generation ethnic networks: structuring academic success of Korean American high school students. In C. C. Park, A. L. Goodwin, & S. J. Lee (Eds.), *Asian American identities, families, and schooling* (pp. 157–176). Greenwich, CT: Information Age Publishing.

Louie, V. S. (2004). *Compelled to excel: Immigration, education, and opportunity among Chinese Americans*. Stanford, CA: Stanford University Press.

Olsen, L. (1997). *Made in America: Immigrant students in our public schools*. New York, NY: New Press.

Phelan, P., Davidson, A. L., & Yu, H. C. (1998). *Adolescents' worlds: Negotiating family, peers, and school*. New York, NY: Teachers College Press.

Piha, S., & Adams, A. (2001). *Youth development guide: Engaging young people in after-school programming*. San Francisco, CA: Community Network for Youth Development. Electronic Document. Retrieved from http://www.cnyd.org/trainingtools/CNYD_YD_Guide.pdf

Reyes, E. E. (1995). Asian Pacific Queer Space. In G. Y. Okihiro, M. Alquizola, D. F. Rony, & K. S. Wong (Eds.), *Privileging positions: The sites of Asian American Studies* (pp. 251–259). Pullman, WA: Washington State University Press.

Suárez-Orozco, C., & Suárez-Orozco, M. M. (2001). *Children of immigration.* Cambridge, MA: Harvard University Press.

Sung, B. L. (1987). *The adjustment experiences of Chinese immigrant children in New York City.* New York, NY: Center for Migration Studies.

Thai, H. C. (2002). Formation of ethnic identity among second-generation Vietnamese Americans. In P. G. Min (Ed.), *The second generation: Ethnic identity among Asian Americans* (pp. 53–83). Walnut Creek, CA: Altamira Press.

Valenzuela, A. (1999). *Subtractive schooling: U.S.-Mexican youth and the politics of caring.* Albany, NY: State of New York Press.

Waters, M. C. (1999). *Black identities: West Indian immigrant dreams and American realities.* Cambridge, MA: Harvard University Press.

Yohalem, N. (2003). Adults who make a difference: Identifying the skills and characteristics of successful youth workers. In F. A. Villarruel, D. F. Perkins, L. M. Borden, & J. G. Keith (Eds.), *Community youth development: Programs, policies, and practices* (pp. 358–372). Thousand Oaks, CA: Sage Publications.

Zhou, M., & Bankston III, C. L. (1998). *Growing up American: How Vietnamese adapt to life in the United States.* New York, NY: Russell Stage Foundation.

CHAPTER SEVEN

Revisiting and reflecting with the CYC youth

In the summer of 2015, I reconnected with seventeen young people. Eight and half years have passed since I last interviewed many of the CYC youth, who at the time were in middle school and high school. Even after the completion of the interviews, I would often see the youth and their families when visiting Harborview. We generally kept in touch via social media. Today, they are all high school graduates and either pursuing higher education or have obtained a bachelor's or graduate degree and working full-time. The young adults still spoke about the importance and significance that CYC has had in their lives as they acclimated to a new country, a new neighborhood, and/or a new school. CYC is, as many expressed, their "second home" and thus "we're family here." The purpose of this chapter is to revisit some of the young people who participated in CYC and are now "CYC alums." The focus group was "a reunion," Jessica expresses, as it was an opportunity to reconnect with many of their peers and reflect on their CYC memories. Furthermore, listening to each other's experiences was like "having flashbacks" to their own CYC memories, adds David.

"I didn't realize I had such a long history with HCCC," reflected twenty-four-year-old Jessica. Growing up, her parents worked long hours and thus needed childcare. Jessica's dad worked in construction and her mom was a beautician in Chinatown. Jessica's mother enrolled her in HCCC's early childcare program, since it was accessible to both their home and her mom's work. Later, Jessica learned about CYC through Wai-Ming and participated in the summer programming during her middle school years. Being a family friend, Wai-Ming's encouragements assisted Jessica's participation and transition to CYC. Today, as a social entrepreneur and toy designer, Jessica credits her success and passion to HCCC's programs and, more importantly, the meaningful relationships she developed *and* maintained with the CYC familial. She explained:

> I feel like my relationships with people at CYC have been most benefiting in terms of the social aspects. When I first started the summer program, I feel super connected with the high school youth staff. I fell in love with them. It was like having a big brother and sister. Being an only child may have something to do with it. Just having role models who were older than you and who had gone through more schooling and knew the whole process of going to college were extremely helpful. It is knowing you had someone there who you could reach out to. Even being able to open up socially was important because I was, and still am, a pretty shy person. CYC allowed me to open up more through participating in the different program opportunities. So I felt that was most valuable.

The importance of "knowing you had someone there" allowed Jessica to "open up more" and explore the various opportunities that CYC offered. As a ninth grader, Jessica decided to give back to CYC, because she appreciated the "sense of home" and "tremendous support" at CYC, particularly since growing up as an only child and her parents working long hours. Throughout her high school career, Jessica tutored at CYC during the academic year and was a teaching assistant in the youth summer arts program. She explained the knowledge and tools that CYC taught her were valuable, "Having that connection with the staffs transferred to how I want to do tutoring. I wanted to be part of that cycle of relationships. What the staffs and older teens provided me, I wanted to continue that cycle with the younger teens." Similar to other young adults, Jessica's desires to give back or "continue that cycle" were due to the "instrumental" role CYC and HCCC has played during her K-12 years. She reflects:

> Being in the tutoring program as a tutor helped me tremendously, because I not only got to contribute to the services of tutoring but I also got a lot out of it, in terms of social skills and being able to interact with students one-on-one. I remember training with [one of the staff] and how they gave the tutors lesson plans. I learned you can't just give them the answers. Instead, you have to challenge them and ask the right questions and not let them depend on you. You have to encourage them to be more independent and to be able to solve and do the homework on their own. I felt that was incredibly helpful for me, because I never thought about it that way. I was just like, 'Oh, I've done homework before. I am good at it. I can be there for students.' But I realized there was so much more to being a tutor. The relationships that came

out of my years as a CYC tutor was very meaningful. I'm connected with [my former tutees] on Facebook. I just saw a graduation photo, so it's really easy to get caught in a flashback. 'Wow, you've grown up so much!'

Jessica explains the skills that she learned as a tutor in CYC were instrumental—even afterward: "I tutored in college and I was able to apply my CYC tutoring experience." Today, in terms of life after college and career opportunities, Jessica explains the importance of reciprocity and being an agent of social change, which she credits CYC:

> I am a social entrepreneur. My friend and I work with schools and organizations in the region. So in that sense, it's community-oriented. I just really appreciate CYC and HCCC being such an amazing resource for the community and having a huge social impact for the Asian American community in Chinatown, especially with all the gentrification that's going on. I just want to continue being a part of a group of people trying to do better in the world. It also got me thinking a lot about how people connect with others, especially I am working with children a lot and doing research for toys as a social entrepreneur. It's really made me more aware of the work that I am doing. For instance, just asking questions and not being completely directive and just letting kids take the lead and seeing where the outcomes go from there. At the same time, framing it with goals in mind so they are on a trajectory of skill development for social, emotional, language or anything they might be working on. My experience in CYC has made me want to do that. I definitely feel having CYC in my life has an influence on what I want to do and crafting this career of combining and starting my own business and also trying to do well in the world is important.

Jessica's narrative illuminates the various forms of community cultural wealth that the youth and their families possess and are able to (re)engage through their involvement with HCCC and other grassroots CBOs in Chinatown. Chapter 7 focuses on the youths' community cultural wealth that HCCC acknowledges and views as assets when working with *and* for the community. As discussed in Chapter 1, community cultural wealth comprises at least six forms of capital: familial, linguistic, social, navigational, aspirational, and resistant.

Familial capital "refers to those cultural knowledges nurtured among familial (kin) that carry a sense of community history, memory, and cultural institution" (Yosso & García, 2007, p. 164). Additionally, familial capital is committed to maintaining a community well-being and includes "a broader understanding of kinship" (p. 164). *Linguistic capital*, as Yosso and García (2007) discussed, "includes the intellectual and social skills attained through communication in multiple languages and/or language styles" (p. 160). As noted in the previous chapters, CYC nurtured and amplified the youths' home languages while providing the capital and codes needed to access and navigate U.S. society. *Aspirational capital* refers to "the ability to maintain hopes and dreams for the future, even in the face of real and perceived barriers" (Yosso, 2005, p. 77). *Social capital* is the "networks of people and community resources" (p. 79) and *navigational capital* "refers to skills of maneuvering through social institutions" (p. 80). *Resistant capital* applies "those knowledges and skills fostered through oppositional behavior that challenges inequality" (p. 80) as noted by Yosso (2005). In addition to providing the knowledge and tools of oppression, the youth developed ways to dismantle and transform such oppressive structures through *transformative resistant capital* (Yosso, 2005).

"Knowing you have someone": Familial and linguistic capitals

Many friendships were established at CYC, and more importantly their friendships still remain. In other words, the youth met at CYC and have maintained those relationships even after CYC, high school, and college. As one of the young adults expresses, "We met here and have been long time friends. Our friendship has been constant." I recall attending many of the youths' high school graduations and there would always be a crowd from CYC. They attended each other's undergraduate and graduate commencements as well as other special life events (e.g., home purchases, weddings, first jobs, etc.). CYC is a second home for the young people because they were able to develop relationships with friends and staff members. Twenty-five-year-old Steven recalls, "Immigrating here [to the U.S.], you definitely have nobody. You have to find somewhere to start. If I didn't have CYC, I wouldn't have the starting point. I met my friends here. CYC was the starting point for me. It was and still definitely an important part of my life." Essentially, the young adults credit CYC in developing many of the friendships. Twenty-one-year-old Yanlin credits CYC for providing a place to meet people and a welcoming space to hangout: "CYC is important as far as providing a place where we met each other and get to hangout. Without CYC, our group of friends and our relationship wouldn't be what it is today. If CYC wasn't here, we wouldn't meet and call each other to hangout." Moreover, the young adults explain how and why CYC is their second home. Samantha adds:

> CYC is a second home for me. A lot of people say this as well. Other than my house, I was here most of the time. The CYC staffs are family—we can go to them for advice. CYC is an important part of my life. I learned most of my English here from speaking to people, especially with Jeff. We were allowed to speak Cantonese and English at the same time. So it's not like we didn't get to practice English or were told we can't speak Cantonese.

As discussed in Chapter 6, CYC respects the youths' home cultures while learning U.S. dominant culture. Today, the young adults maintain and engage with their home languages (e.g., Cantonese, Fujianese, Mandarin, Toisanese, etc.) and English (i.e., code switch).

Twenty-six-year-old Tommy, who is an accountant at a private firm, reflects on his experience with CYC:

> CYC and HCCC are my second home. I started coming to CYC when I was in 5th grade, really young. My friend introduced me to CYC. I didn't know anyone here. I was a pretty mischievous child. I met a lot of people at CYC. My family knew CYC as an afterschool program, so they didn't need to worry about me during the non-school hours. Every day after school, I would get off the school bus and walk across the street to CYC. I also learned many things and people would tutor me if I needed help on my homework. I was surrounded by a lot of positive people. As a result, I obtained a lot of positive life perspectives. For example, there were times when I wanted to give up and didn't want to pursue something, because it was too hard. They would always encourage and support me. There were a lot of workshops, like the effects of smoking. Even though I have friends outside of CYC that smoked, I didn't do it. So CYC has a positive influence and outlook in life.

Kevin, who we met in Chapter 6, elaborates on how society enforces "a lot of pressures and stresses," particularly as an immigrant and an Asian American, but CYC has always provided a positive and much needed outlet for him:

> CYC was very positive for me. There was no peer pressure to do anything. This is very important, because there's a lot of pressure and stress outside of CYC. People would say to you, 'You need to do this and do that.' Here at CYC, there's none of that pressure. People would encourage you to try something new, but not pressuring. It's just a very positive space. It allowed me to try and pursue different activities. If I like it then I can continue. And if I don't, then at least I tried it and had fun. This was very important.

During his high school career, Kevin became involved with the CYC band and the youth leadership programs. Having never played a musical instrument and participated in performances, being in the band was "very rewarding" and he always looked forward to it. His parents supported Kevin's participation at CYC since "they noticed I have become a lot happier because I had a social life and not just academics. After I started coming to CYC, my mom noticed a change in me, that I am more involved in the community and doing more youth activities. She was happy for me."

Additionally, Ling illuminates the intergenerational gap between many Asian American youth and their immigrant elders, especially during middle and high school. As a result, "CYC provided us a place to do activities, meet people and do things after school, instead of hanging out somewhere. Knowing there's a place for us to hangout instead of making possible bad choices is important." Later, Ling expresses a profound appreciation for CYC:

> I am thankful for the friendships that I was able to build at CYC. Also, I am a person that enjoys really deep conversations. Some of the memories that I remember were having these deep conversations with the staffs. I was able to talk about serious stuff with them. It was really enjoyable. I will always remember them.

Michelle adds, "If you go to another organization, they may not have that kind of support group that CYC offers. CYC was a place that people talked about, 'Let's go to CYC. CYC has this and CYC has that'."

The staffs' authentic caring and passion were strong qualities expressed by the young adults. Furthermore, as discussed in Chapters 4 and 5, cultural relevant understanding is important when working with youth and their families. Throughout the focus groups, the young adults repeated "passionate" in describing the CYC staffs. Amy explains what passionate means for her:

> The way I define passionate is the way the staffs care, the way they follow-up, and the way they spend time. They remember when the A, B, C things that happen in your life. They don't see this as just a job. They see this as a family. When the youth are coming in, the staffs are greeting their brothers and sisters. It's like coming to a family, instead of 'I am the staff.' They care. It's that caring that makes you feel like you are actually wanted here and that's a very important part because most part of my teenage years, I just want to fit in, whether it be at school or here. It's time that is special and unique … Also, adults usually see teenagers as 'they are up to no good.' However, it's different here. The staffs always see the good in us. It makes you feel comfortable. It makes you feel that they actually have trust in me; and that I am a good person.

Amy's point that "the staffs always see the good in us" and "that I am a good person" is important to mention, particularly since young people of color are often viewed as dangerous, deficit, and a problem in society. On the other hand, the CYC staffs view the youth as their family and amplify their assets and cultural wealth. Calvin follows up with explaining the staffs' passion guided him in deciding his focus in college and as a career. He states:

> One thing I got from all the CYC staffs is being passionate on what you do in life. All the staffs are very passionate about what they are doing, like welcoming us and being there for us. The staffs are there if you need them. They take that extra mile. They reach out instead of sitting there and waiting for you to come. That's my idea of passion. So deciding on my major in college was a very personal thing. If I really

wanted to get into this, I have to love it and be very passionate. I learned that from being in CYC. I always come back during breaks and talk to them about college life and personal things. They are willing to listen.

Connie shares having staffs who are also children of immigrants was a strength since they have lived through similar experiences: "If there's any personal things, anything going bad then you are able to go to somebody to share because they are also from immigrant families. If I try to tell my mom, she would be like, 'I have no idea what you are talking about'." The importance of "passion" that the CYC staffs transpired to the young adults' outlook in life is worth noting, particularly with their career possibilities. As children of immigrants, the ability to figure out and decide on their careers is something that many of their immigrant elders typically do not have the option and privilege to do in the United States. This is especially true for individuals who are immigrants of color, low-income and working-poor, have limited English abilities, and need to support a family. Instead, as I illuminated in Chapter 3, immigrants quite often experience downward mobility and/or are limited to working long insidious hours in low-wage positions. As a result, children of immigrants may not easily translate their elders' hardships and survival as a form of passion. Or immigrant elders may not readily acknowledge the sense of passion that many young adults shared.

The staffs' willingness to listen and provide authentic caring was an important element that Yanlin shares as well. Yanlin just finished her second year of college in nursing when we met up in June of 2015. She immigrated to the United States at the age of nine with her parents and brother. Both her parents work in ethnic restaurants. Yanlin was enrolled in a bilingual fifth grade classroom. Two years later, she began coming to CYC when her best friend Samantha told her about the academic and enrichment programs. Yanlin enjoyed being in the bilingual fifth classroom, especially since that is where she and Samantha met. Their teacher, Ms. Chan, was a bilingual speaker and understood the challenges of learning a new culture. Thus, Yanlin felt comfortable and enjoyed school. Things started to change for Yanlin in sixth grade. She started middle school. The school did not have a bilingual program and while she and Samantha were in the same school, they rarely saw each other during the school hours. Yanlin stopped going to school in sixth and seventh grade, because "I was lost. I wasn't ready to accept that I was here in the U.S." Additionally, Yanlin conveys of never having meaningful relationships with her school staffs, which added to her disassociation with school. She says:

I never had a close relationship with my teachers, like I couldn't go to them and talk. Sometimes I feel teachers don't care enough to come to me, to check in with me. I remember when I was in trouble in middle school; they weren't the ones to come talk with me. No one came. It was actually the guidance counselor that came, but I barely met and never talked to the counselor before then. The counselor called my mom to come to the school. My mom didn't speak English so I translated for my mom. They were trying to get me to go back to school. I was just so angry back then. I feel like the school needed to talk to me, but they didn't. So I didn't listen. I just stayed home.

Yanlin's guidance counselor later contacted child services, which led to anxiety and caused a lot of misunderstanding and distrust for her family with U.S. schools. She explains:

They wanted to take me away from my parents. They were like "you're not letting your child go to school". But that was me not wanting to go, not my parents. So they were going to take me away and my mom was so scared. I guess my counselor contacted my teachers from before and so Ms. Chan, my fifth grade teacher, came. Ms. Chan was the only teacher that was there to talk to me about stuff. Ms. Chan and the CYC staff told my school 'don't do that'. Let us talk to her and work this out, instead of getting child services involved. Ms. Chan talked to my mom and me. The CYC staffs were there to talk to me and always checked in with me. If my parents, especially my mom, didn't have that support from them, they would be lost. My mom didn't know anything about the U.S. system. We were farmers, so we didn't know much. I would say Ms. Chan and CYC helped my mom out a lot.

Yanlin also adds:

Back then I didn't want to be in the U.S. So the whole time, I was like, "Mom, can we just go back?" My mom cried. My parents had a lot of people come talk to me. They had my cousin, who was born here, talk to me. Then they had another cousin, who wasn't born here, talk to me. I was really stubborn. I thought they didn't understand me. They just kept telling me to go back to school. Ms. Chan told me to go to school and she was like, "If you really want to go back in the summer, I will pay for your ticket to go back." She was a really great teacher. From my experience, I would say Chinese teachers definitely care more about their students. They know we are immigrants and we are struggling so they try to help [with the transition].

Since Yanlin and Samantha also did not attend and skipped CYC academic programs, they agree the CYC staffs "cared a lot about us" and "got us back to CYC." Yanlin realized the significance of an education when doctors found a tumor in her dad. They were able to remove the tumor, but the experience altered Yanlin's outlook and she quickly realized "I needed to grow up," thus "I got back on my feet and changed."

After the experience, Yanlin reflects on how her teachers did not provide a supportive environment when she returned to school. Instead, she felt her teachers' perceptions of her turned negative and unwelcoming:

The look that the teachers gave me when I decided to go back to school, it's like they think I am a bad kid. I am not sure if they intended to welcome me back, but that's not the vibe that I was getting. It wasn't just one teacher. It was all of my teachers. I guess they didn't know what to do with me. They gave me a vibe that they don't want to deal with me, so they didn't even say anything like "welcome back" or "I'm happy that you're back." They just gave me this look. It's like they don't want to get involved and deal with things. I think as a teacher, it's part of your job to help guide the student. I feel I didn't get that support back then in middle school. The school staffs are not comparable to the CYC staff.

Samantha agrees:

The relationship we have with the CYC staffs is stronger than with the school staffs. It's just not the same. I feel the relationship we have with the teachers and school staffs is very surface level. But CYC is different. We're able to bond more. The CYC staffs really care. They always ask us what's going on. We are more comfortable to tell the staffs things. So there's a stronger bond between the CYC staffs and us.

Yanlin and Samantha explain how school educators could better support children of immigrants, particularly recent immigrants, as they adjust to various new lifestyles. Similarly, many of the young adults shared the CYC staffs did not just connected with the youth, but also with their family like siblings, parents, and other family members. As a result, CYC acknowledges the youth and their families in developing *and* maintaining trust as well as familial and linguistic capitals.

"The staffs broaden my views": Social and navigational capitals

As highlighted in Chapter 6, the young people expressed their parents expected them to pursue higher education. In other words, higher education was a necessity to achieving a stable life—a life that immigrant parents are unable to achieve due to the language barrier. "Parents don't want you to end up working in restaurants," commented Ling, since these jobs are often low paying and strenuous. "Parents sacrificed so much to come here. They left their life back in China and then they come here and work so hard. College opens up more opportunities for you." The parents' sacrifice motivates the young people to push and continue their education, no matter what barriers arise. In other words, children of immigrants display a strong sense of resiliency even during difficult times. A young adult explains:

For the parents, it wasn't like "get an education so you can take care of us in the future." It's more like, "we came here because we want you to have a better future then what we had in China." They sacrifice for us by coming to the U.S. and staying in a land where they don't know the language. In a sense, you want to give back to your family by pursuing a higher education and finishing high school and college. It's an understood message.

Another young adult reflected on the hardships that their parents endure:

> They work so hard. They work everyday just for us to have a life here. Before I didn't realize how hard it is to make money. I would just ask my parents for money everyday. We always buy tons of snacks. When you spend the money, you don't necessary watch your spending. You just ask your parents for money when you run out. Later on, I realized how hard they work. They come home and they are always exhausted. My mom always has sore arms. It breaks my heart to watch them come home everyday exhausted like that. CYC always encourages us to talk to the staff, like if we ever need anything the staffs are here. They would also encourage us to talk to our parents. That's how I realized my parents' hard work.

The parents' resiliency transferred to the young adults' lives. In other words, in times of real and perceived challenges, the young adults are able to maintain hope and dreams for the future since their parents' hard work and sacrifice are forms of encouragements and perseverance. The CYC staff, also children of immigrant, shares with the youth the importance of reaching out to their elders.

At the same time, while immigrant families value education, they are unable to provide their children the guidance needed to translate those dreams into reality, as noted by Louie (2004). I will illustrate how community-based organizations, like CYC, offer social and navigational capitals for low-income immigrant families in achieving and preparing our young people. Samantha summarized what many young adults shared about CYC's presence in the community, "CYC helped prepare us for life after high school."

College access initiative

Calvin just finished his second year of college when we reconnected in summer 2015. During his junior and senior year of high school, Calvin participated in CYC's college access initiative where he was paired up with a volunteer mentor. As a first generation college student, he explained how CYC helped him navigate through the college application process:

> CYC helped me 100% with the college application. My mentor helped me out with FAFSA, applications, essays, supplements, and basically everything I had any questions. My mentor helped me a lot. We would set up our own schedule, such as when should this be completed and when should we brainstorm and finalize the documents. He's very cool. Every time we meet up, we would go grab food and talk about college

and high school stuff. It's nice to be able to talk to someone who has gone through the process. I learned a lot.

Samantha, also a first generation college student, explained the benefits of having a college mentor while she was going through the application process:

> My mentor got me through the college process and with everything else. I could talk to her about anything because they know it all. I can't go to my parents because they don't know anything about the college process. So I need that person who I can go to. The school counselors are always busy. They have a lot of students, so it's hard to meet with them. So it's good to have a mentor, like someone who can provide you one-on-one.

Similar to other research (Teranishi, 2010), the accessibility to counselors was a challenge for many of the young adults. Many spoke of the meetings either "being very brief" or "rushed," thus the student–counselor relationships often were "impersonal." Others also expressed scheduling a meeting with their guidance counselors was difficult. When Tommy tried to meet with his guidance counselor to discuss higher education options, scheduling a time was a challenge, now able to reflect with a laugh:

> While I have a guidance counselor, I didn't get much support from them. I stopped by their office, but my guidance counselor would tell me to set-up an appointment. When I look at the sign-up sheet, all of the appointment slots were already taken. There were no openings at all. I was like, 'Wow, really, all of the appointment slots are already taken up!'

In addition to the college mentor program, the young adults spoke of the importance of CYC's college tours. As first generation college students, they value the accessibility that CYC offered and having a trusting relationship with the staff was crucial. Steven brought up accessibility as an important factor with the college tours. His parents work at an Asian supermarket that does not provide flexible hours. The college tours provided him and others an opportunity to see the different campuses and ask the respective representatives questions. Steven explains:

> One of the colleges that I was considering is three hours away and in the middle of nowhere. My parents have to work and my dad is the only one who drove back then. He has to work on the weekends, too. I actually decided to attend the university that I graduated from as a result of the CYC tour. The tour helped me before I submitted my application. I got to see the campus and experience the college life, which was good. If it wasn't for CYC, there's no way for us to go on college tours.

Jessica also shared if CYC did not offer the college tours, she would not have had the opportunity to visit the various campuses since her parents cannot afford to leave work. Moreover, as the first in her family to apply and pursue higher education, Jessica valued the college access program.

> I just would never have gone and visited college campuses if CYC didn't introduced and offered the college tours. I don't have to concern my mom with taking time off from work. I couldn't convince my mom to drive two hours to go to a random school that we may or may not consider as a viable option. I can come back with a report and photos and tell her about the trip. Especially being a first generation college student, you don't even know what kinds of questions to ask even if you do end up on campus tours. Being introduced to that through CYC was really helpful, just to be able to learn what to look for and how to get the most out of a tour. Just having something that's so organized and informative was really helpful and accessible.

Likewise, David shared "there were a lot of things that I personally didn't know or what kind of things to look for" when applying to college. "I knew there were certain things that I would like to see, but at the same time, college was new to me." Many expressed the CYC staffs "know you as a person" rather than simply a statistic, which helped to figure out which type of higher education institutions suits them. David said:

> It's hard to explain to my parents what is a good college for me, when I myself have some things that I am not so sure about. But having somebody who been to college as your guide and someone who's gone through those experiences and to actually know you as a person is very important. The CYC staff would help you look at the situation and decide if this place is the right place for you. The most challenging part of the overall college application process was writing the essay. It's hard. It's a very personal message that you are trying to express to your school. They always ask a very generic question, like something that's important to you or something that changed your life. You can write it, but who's going to read it? You want someone who can give you an honest feedback. Your parents won't be able to do it. Well, my parents can't. My parents don't know enough English. Even if I explain it to them, they won't know the grammar and tone. Everything is just different on paper. So having the CYC staffs being the reviewer of the work that I did for colleges and them knowing me personally and understanding this was a very personal message to try to get into a school. Their critique was key to the whole process.

Monumental enrichment memories

CYC offered a space for young people to experience a variety of enrichment activities as well as things beyond Chinatown. For example, the CYC band provided the youth an outlet to learn and appreciate music and the arts, particularly since many schools did not offer such classes. Samantha was in the CYC band for five years and appreciated having the opportunity to be a part of the group:

CYC really want us to improve because we are all so passionate about music. So they really looked to see who is good out there and then found the really good teachers to teach us.

Anna also reflected on her experience with the CYC band, particularly valuing the one-on-one peer mentoring process:

The band was just real. There were older teens, so they were teaching us. So it was really friendly. If you don't know how to play, the staff would have the older teens teach you one-on-one, and then everyone come together to practice.

Moreover, many of the young adults shared they went on their first outings with CYC—e.g., movies, amusement parks, beach, and camping trips. David mentioned. "I went to my first camping trip with CYC. I went to see my first movie ever. It was Bugs Life. Being here, I got to experience a lot of things that I wouldn't have if I stayed at home all day long. I wouldn't have been able to get the full rich experience." Jessica added the importance of having the enrichment opportunities since they were "monumental moments in my life":

I didn't realize they were such monumental moments in my life. Since CYC, I haven't been camping. So that was my one and only camping trip. Amusement parks, I remember going every year, but after CYC, I never went again. It was a really incredible resource to get out and experience things that I would not have had the opportunity if it were not for CYC. My mom works and would not be able to take me to amusement parks. It's awesome having all those clubs, too. I remember rollerblading club that Jeff organized. I still have the scar from when I fell, but it was still a lot of fun to just explore the city on wheels. Otherwise, I would have never done that alone. It's really awesome to have this community of people to do things.

"I have a voice to do something positive for the community": Aspirational and resistant capitals

"Giving back to the community" was resonated during all of the focus group sessions with the young adults. Their desires to give back highlighted the significant role CYC has played in their lives, particularly regarding aspirational and resistant capitals. They recognized the passion and dedication of the staff. For instance, CYC's tutoring program is all-volunteer run. While there are a few who respond to the fliers, the majority of the tutors are high school and college students who were former tutees at CYC because, as Cindy (CYC Tutoring Coordinator) expressed, the youth want to "give back to the community." They recognize the importance and benefits of CYC's tutoring program because they received academic support and resources from the tutors and staff. For instance, Steven was a tutee for three years and then was a tutor throughout his years in high school. He became a tutor because "I wanted to help the younger teens who are in middle school. I got the help when I needed it before." Both David and Huifen became tutors at CYC because of their appreciation for CYC, particularly Cindy's dedication to the tutoring program. "I wanted to give back and help out Cindy," explains David, "because she was the person who was always there when I needed help with homework. It taught me a lot of things. Now that I have the ability to do my own homework, I wanted to give back." Likewise, Huifen voices:

> When I learned you need community service in high school and for college applications, the first thing that I thought of was I could tutor at CYC to give back. If I have the opportunity to volunteer at school or CYC, without a doubt I would choose CYC because they have provided me a lot of resources and support and so it's a good way to contribute back.

In addition to the tutoring program, the youth viewed the youth leadership program as an important component. CYC's youth leadership program, Michelle explains, is "training youth leaders to be a role model to other youth while learning skills and practicing them through different workshops and programs." For instance, reflecting on what she took away from the program: "it was a place for me to work with other youth who were equally passionate about learning different issues that would make a difference in their friend groups and also within the community," noted Michelle. She summed up her relationship with CYC and HCCC.

> CYC has been a very good place to me. My family life began to blend with CYC. My brother was involved with HCCC because he has special needs. My mom attended the Family Service & Support workshops. She met other parents who have children with special needs. They would share resources and network. So right now, my whole family is involved with HCCC. I try to give back as much as I can.

Likewise, many young adults also spoke highly of the youth leadership program. As I will show, the program offered them leadership skills, public speaking, time management, confidence, and Asian American studies.

Kevin graduated from a private university in 2013. When we reconnected in 2015, he was a researcher at a local medical institution. In the near future, he hopes to pursue medical school and become a pediatric doctor, which has always been his childhood dream. Kevin describes himself as "activist." He credits CYC for providing him the knowledge and tools to understand and address the injustices that face immigrants of color, particularly Asian Americans. Through participating in

CYC's leadership programs during his high school career, Kevin decided to take Asian American studies courses in college to continue his growth. He explains:

> I am studying medicine now, but through CYC I am also an activist. There was an activism component that I gained a lot of understanding of the issues facing our communities. In college, I became more aware and understanding of my culture and the problems that Asian Americans and immigrants face. For example, many people don't understand the model minority as well as discrimination and racism that Asians face. In college, I took more classes and attended workshops about the model minority and the Asian American community.

I asked Kevin why is there a need for Asian American studies courses and to be engaged with community activism. He expressed a sense of responsibility to serve and fight for communities that often are silenced, muted, and ignored by dominant society. Kevin mentions:

> Before, in the past, I didn't care about the community. In the beginning, I didn't understand why these issues were so important. But when I became involved with the leadership program, I realized everyone is affected. You may not live here, but we are all connected. Your parents live here. And there are so many people around you. For me, it is important for me to speak up, particularly for those people who can't speak out. I want to speak up and let people know the issues that are happening in the community so we can fight for the causes. It's important to understand the issues that are happening in Chinatown.

Kevin also emphasizes the dangers of a single story (Adichie, 2009) and master narrative of U.S. history (Takaki, 2008). Chimamanda Ngozi Adichie (2009) "warns that if we hear only a single story about another person or country, we risk a critical misunderstanding." At the same time, Adichie explains understanding how power works is essential:

> It is impossible to talk about the single story without talking about power. How they are told, who tells them, when they're told, how many stories are told, are really dependent on power. Power is the ability not just to tell the story of another person, but to make it the definitive story of that person.

In order to acknowledge the diversity of Asian Americans, it is necessary to disaggregate the data. If we reduce people to a single story, we are essentially taking away their humanity. In other words, we are dehumanizing the individual(s). Kevin states the importance of dismantling the single story throughout our curriculum and everyday lives:

There are so many Asians. It's so important for people to understand the Asian and Asian American struggles, because schools don't focus much on Asian and Asian American communities. I would love to see an expansion of learning—a more holistic approach and diverse curriculum to teach students about the different topics that Asian and Asian American face. Even in high school, you don't really learn about Asian and Asian Americans. Maybe the California gold rush, but that's it. Even in Harborview, there's so many issues that Asians face, but we don't hear about it. I didn't learn about it or the history of Chinatown until I came to CYC. For me, I would like to learn about the Asian diaspora in the U.S. and how the struggles have shaped our nation. It's very important. When there's something about Asian and Asian American, the coverage in the news is so little. It's sad that our voice don't get heard. I really want to see more of that and activism in our community.

Through his involvements in the CYC's leadership program, Kevin's conscientization (Freire, 1999, 2005) of the injustices and the institutions that maintain inequalities (Ore, 2003) blossomed. "Before, I hear about it, but didn't really care about it, explains Kevin." "I didn't understand what it has to do with me. One year we were organizing to open a library branch in Chinatown. Initially, I didn't understand why we needed one because there's one in another neighborhood. I didn't understand the meaning behind it." Through participating in the youth leadership program, Kevin's awareness of injustices became clear and realized he *is* an agent of change. He shares:

> Then I realized all of the neighborhoods have a library, except Chinatown. So that was a very important step for me to understand about the problems that Chinatown is experiencing. It made me realize I have a voice and I want to use my voice to do something positive and to create change for the people in my community. I want to give back to the community. For me, this is very important.

Since working at the medical institution, Kevin learned many multilingual immigrants of color are often disconnected with the U.S. medical system. He explains while there may be translation services available, the medical understanding is lacking. "The patients don't understand what it all means," he explains. "For example, the translators don't explain what's anemia and brain cancer." As a result, he wants to be a medical profession that explains to his patients, rather than saying "your only options are either go to chemotherapy or you die and then move on. I don't want to be that kind of doctor." Kevin elaborates:

> There are a lot of doctors here that don't give enough time to the immigrant populations. I see especially for the Asian population, the medical staffs treat them pretty badly. I just want to change the medical system in the immigrant population. I want to be able to explain to them these services, such as Medicare and Medicaid, as well

as their symptoms. So I want to be the kind of doctor that explains to my patients so they can better understand medicine.

Similarly, Michelle echoes the importance of giving back to the community:

I also picked up the activist spirit. When I was in CYC, I joined the Mayor's Youth Advisory through the encouragement of the staffs. In my application, I remember saying I want to be a voice for my community, because I live here and I benefited from the resources. I want to be a part of that. I wanted to raise awareness. So I did that in high school. And then going into college, I continue to find myself in situations like Kevin where I have to speak up or expose people to certain issues that people may not know. For instance, gentrification is a concern facing Chinatown. I took a video art class in college and for my final project I decided to capture stories. I am very hungry for stories so throughout the whole semester I tried to learn the skills to capture stories. I interviewed the residents who were evicted from their apartments and then I put together a video to expose people to gentrification. For me, that's a way for me to say I love art and I also love social advocacy. So how can I combine the two together? That was one of the examples. I also love poetry, so I write poetries to share with people at spoken word events and poetry slams so they know what I go through as an Asian American. And as an individual, I want to care about people in marginalized communities.

Becky adds having a place and space to learn leadership skills, public speaking, and Asian American experiences is crucial since dominant society quite often forces youth of color to abandon their cultures and identities. She participated in another youth leadership program in Chinatown, but found it similar to CYC while others shared their narratives. Becky remarked:

Middle school was a very confusing time for me because, as a 13 and 14 year old, I was experiencing an identity crisis. I was figuring out who I am. Am I Chinese or Chinese American? What's the difference? So I was very confused. As a high school youth in the program, I learned about Asian American history and issues, such as affordable housing. Being in the youth program allowed me to grow and be comfortable with myself. The program really helped me when I was having my identity crisis. I am also able to articulate what's Asian American for me.

Being a part of youth leadership programs like CYC also provided the youth research and teamwork skills. Tommy explains:

The youth leadership is a place where you gain the knowledge and then pass it on to the next generation. I learned how to do research and how to work as a team with other members. And then what you learned from conducting the research, your team would have a workshop to teach the younger generation. I try to give back from what I learned here as a youth. The staffs are my role models and so I try to do what the staff have taught me and pass it to the next generation so the youth have the opportunities that I gained from the staff. It's not about taking the resources and then I go and leave. CYC is your home and so you should help your siblings (i.e., the younger teens). You don't want them to miss out on things. Before I joined the CYC leadership program, my time was very unproductive. I was quite shy. I am more talkative now, but back then I was quiet and reserved. I didn't know what to do when I got up in front of others. My confidence increased as I did more public speaking in front of large audiences. You are able to express yourself more easily instead of being shy.

Many of the young adults explained that the purpose of facilitating the workshops was to be comfortable speaking in front of others. Furthermore, the young adults spoke of gaining confidence and leadership skills, which are important as they start their careers. Tommy shared to the group the impact CYC's youth leadership program had on his professional and social circles:

I highly credit CYC, since the program helped me in my work life and social life. When I go on interviews, I am more relaxed and confident. One more thing that the program taught me is working with diverse people. In the youth leadership program, we worked with our peers on deciding a topic and then conducting the necessary research. There was a lot of teamwork. Today, when I talk to my co-workers, I am able to express myself and get my points across. It shows management that I am capable of leading a group on projects. The program has taught me so many skills.

Amy admits the skills she learned in the youth leadership program have greatly benefited her; particularly as an architect, she needs to collaborate with various stakeholders and clients. Reflecting, Amy summed it up this way:

It taught me a lot of lifelong skills and how to excel in an environment that you don't know about. I've carried those skills all throughout my whole life. Skills like public speaking and being comfortable in your own skin. It's not just about public speaking, which is only one element of it. It's also about holding yourself and each other accountable: you being on time, you keeping up on your task, you doing your work and you present your work and not being shy and speaking your mind. It's taught me how to present, research, and write and just talk about essential things like critical thinking and public speaking as well as how to lead a team and how to direct the members to do the right things and the right path to achieve a workshop for example. The program prepares you for a lot of things and has taught me a lot about myself. It shapes you as an individual. So it's full circle.

Furthermore, several young adults chose their careers as a way to give back to the community. Amy elaborates on her decision to pursue architecture, specifically focusing on mixed-income housing developments:

I lived in government housing so that's something I see and remember. I want to do something about it. So I became an architect. There's a specific field that I chose, which is mixed-income housing for families. I've been focusing on that and the firm that I work for does a lot of work in the city. This is something that the city is struggling with. I am in a research group that does micro-housing, so smaller footage. I'm researching having smaller square footage but still being livable so people can have lower rent. This is my own way of giving back. The importance of housing for people that lives here, the residents, is something that I want to help with and contribute. I just finished a 200 plus housing unit in the middle of the city. I am very happy to see there is actually mixed-income housing in there. I always tell people I want to use my profession to give back to my community. This is something that is important for me. I want to give back to the CYC that I remembered. It's a way of saying I appreciate what they did for me and what kind of person I have become, because of all the people and programs that have contributed to my education and personal growth. Being with CYC and knowing the importance of connecting with the community is important to me. So that's what drives me.

Ling started coming to CYC in high school as a tutor. She expressed her desires to give back and contribute to the next generation and recent immigrants are important goals:

HCCC and CYC and other community-based organizations that I've joined are all trigger points for what I want to do in the future. Participating in CYC tutoring made me realize that I want to help kids who recently immigrated to the U.S. I want to help people that were in the same situation as I was before. I want to help them, especially kids. I was in high school when I started coming to CYC, and I was there to help others as a tutor. So reflecting back, I wish I knew of CYC earlier. I wish someone was able to give me a hand when I struggled with getting accustom to life in the U.S. Although I never received that, I want to be there for others. Making sure they have help and being able to establish a life in the U.S. When people come here to the U.S., they either try to learn really hard and get used to the life in the U.S. or others just give up. I had friends who picked both paths. It just sucks when certain people go on a wrong path and they just give up. Recently, I bumped into an elementary friend of mine. He kind of gave up on his life. I see him doing drugs. If someone was there to help him, maybe he wouldn't have taken that path. Not just having a mentor, but knowing someone they can turn to who can help them. I feel that sense of security is important when you first come to a new place that is a totally different environment. All of these experiences led me to what I want to do in the future. It definitely trigger that passion within me.

In addition to pursuing predominately White institutions (PWIs), the young adults vocalized the wealth disparities that they directly experienced. As a result, many experienced the socioeconomic class and racial structures that exist and thus maintain inequality. Betty just finished her second year in business at a large private university. She shared many of her peers are "born into well off families, like parents who own companies, law firm partners, or CEO of banks." Jessica also illuminated the wealth inequality between her and her peers:

> I realized a lot of the students were really well off. At one point for our final project, one student had to bring his furniture project home and it was this huge table. Someone asked him how he was going to bring it home, because he lived all the way in [another state]. He said, 'oh no, my uncle is just going to fly in with his private helicopter.'

Steven echoed his college experience of the wealth inequality between him and his roommate: "I was talking to my roommate about how I needed to re-apply for scholarships every year. He didn't know anything about scholarships, because his parents are paying out of pocket. There's quite a difference in terms of our experience." For young people who attend(ed) PWIs, they acknowledged CYC for preparing them for such institutions. For example, many mentioned the youth leadership program introduced them to oppressions and privileges.

When Kevin first started college, he quickly realized his peers were all from upper middle class and upper class households. "Everybody has Chanel, Hugo Boss, and all name brands. Sometimes they ask you to go to a very expensive restaurant. Instead of spending $10 or $20, you spend $400 on a meal," he shared. Initially feeling discouraged and an outsider, Kevin shared his concerns and experience with Jeff. He will always remember Jeff's advice, which is "be yourself" and "just be honest." Kevin appreciates the support from Jeff and other CYC staffs throughout his educational career. At the same time, several shared how they always needed to educate their White peers and professors. Michelle elaborated:

> I took a class on adolescent psychology and a lot of the study results were based on middle-class White population. So I was like what about Asian Americans or other marginalized communities? What about their experience? On the feedback at the end of the class, I wrote how I was unsatisfied with the way how my teacher presented the curriculum because she is a middle to upper-middle class White woman who was teaching to a group of middle-upper class Catholic White students. In class, I try to give them different examples. Some of the examples made them feel like, "what world did you come from?" I would tell them, I had a friend who went into prostitution because she needed the money. They were really surprised. Some of those things are the reality that a lot of minorities have to go through. So it was tough and sometimes you are the only one in class that has to do that. ... Whenever I feel discouraged, I was like 'I was a leader at CYC. I am going to be a leader in this class. I am going to speak up.' So it's great we have a training ground here at HCCC. It's a comfort that I can always fall back on.

144 | OPENING DOORS

Michelle's experience is a reminder that students of color are not responsible to educate their White peers and professors about privilege and oppression. Instead, higher education institutions need people who are knowledgeable and committed to educating our students and the wider community.

Conclusion

Reflecting with the young adults reveals a rich illustration of how CBOs like HCCC have played a crucial role in the holistic well-being for children of immigrants from low-income and working-class backgrounds. Chapter 7 also amplified the various forms of community cultural wealth that the youth and their families possess and are able to (re)engage through their involvement with HCCC and other grassroots CBOs in Chinatown.

Works cited

Adichie, C. N. (2009). The danger of a single story. *TED Talk.*

Freire, P. (1999). *Pedagogy of the oppressed.* New York, NY: The Continuum Publishing.

Freire, P. (2005). *Education for critical consciousness.* New York, NY: Continuum International Publishing Group.

Louie, V. S. (2004). *Compelled to excel: Immigration, education, and opportunity among Chinese Americans.* Stanford, CA: Stanford University Press.

Ore, T. E. (2003). Maintaining inequalities: Systems of oppression and privilege. In T. E. Ore (Ed.), *The social construction of difference and inequality: Race, class, gender, and sexuality* (2nd ed., pp. 182–204). New York, NY: McGraw Hill.

Takaki, R. (2008). *A different mirror: A history of multicultural America.* New York, NY: Back Bay Books/Little, Brown, and Co.

Teranishi, R. T. (2010). *Asians in the ivory tower: Dilemmas of racial inequality in American higher education.* New York, NY: Teachers College Press.

Yosso, T. (2005). Whose culture has capital? A critical race theory discussion of community cultural wealth. *Race, Ethnicity and Education, 8*(1), 69–91.

Yosso, T., & García, D. (2007). "This is no slum!": A critical race theory analysis of community cultural wealth in culture clash's Chavez Ravine. *Aztlan: A Journal of Chicano studies, 32*(1), 145–179.

CHAPTER EIGHT

Implication for policy and practice

Throughout this book I have shown how young people and their immigrant families who identified U.S. schools and other institutions as difficult to navigate and negotiate find the services and support at community-based organizations (CBOs) valuable. Instead of viewing the youth and their immigrant families as cultural deficit, HCCC acknowledges and embraces their cultural wealth, and thus serves as a resource in the community. Within HCCC, CYC is a space for youth to acknowledge, maintain, and build upon their community cultural wealth. Thus, what makes HCCC and CYC significant and successful is having a culturally relevant understanding of the community that they serve. In doing so, they have also maintained a sense of a trusting relationship that emphasizes working for *and* with the community. Opening doors is central to HCCC and CYC's work in the community and its something they choose to do. CYC serves as a bridge for the young people and their families because they understand the youths' parents have limited English skills, a limited understanding about how the U.S. school system works, and a limited amount of free time due to long and tiresome work hours in low-paying jobs. For instance, CYC is able to work with the youth and their families in helping them negotiate and navigate with schools, society, and their families—the type of information that middle class and upper middle class students are able to receive at home. In this way, grassroots CBOs, like CYC, are able to offer the necessary resources to families who are not receiving the support from other institutions (e.g., schools). Repeatedly, the young adults expressed the importance CYC has on them and their families. Yanlin, Ling, Becky, and Michelle eloquently explain the need for CBOs:

New immigrants don't know anybody here. So if none of these organizations existed, then who's going to fight for them and help them? So organizations like HCCC are necessary. They're a resource for the people.

—YANLIN

It's really important to have community-based organizations within the community, because immigrant families can turn to these organizations for help. The CBOs help them get used to life in the U.S., so it's really important. You need that in any community, because they have no one to turn to. Knowing there is an organization that they can turn to for help is important. It doesn't matter if it's for yourself, your kids, or family members. There are CBOs that help adults find jobs beside restaurant work, like teaching them computer skills and technical skills. CBOs are the middle person because they bridge the families and society. In terms of schools, CBOs help you understand where both sides are coming from. The school may not know what's going on with the student. And because of language barrier, the student and family don't know what is going on in schools. As a result, the gap widens. Having these CBOs will close off these gaps. So it's important.

—LING

I believe having nonprofit community-based organizations are very important for the community. These nonprofit organizations have a huge impact on my own life. In the beginning, I was involved and introduced to CYC and then got involved with another CBO in Chinatown. I have the opportunity to share my experiences growing up in this community. Chinatown is not simply a place to go for food and restaurants, but there are a lot of cultures and narratives. Chinatown is an important place because it provides a sense of family and community. We need a sense of community, especially with gentrification happening. I hope people will not forget how and why Chinatown began.

—BECKY

I can't imagine a world without community-based organizations, because that's where all the resources are available, so people can come and get help. HCCC is high quality. The staffs are so invested in our lives—not just our lives, but our family as well. HCCC really lives out the quote, 'It takes a village to raise a child'. There is always a sense of village here. We are family. We grew up together. We share the same stories.

—MICHELLE

This book also challenges the portrayal of Asian Americans as model minorities who do not face any barriers. Particularly, how the stereotype of Asian Americans as high-achieving, passive, and accommodating erases their diversity and allows policy makers as well as service providers to ignore many of their basic needs. While some of the youth at CYC maintained passing grades, others struggled in school. Additionally, there is an urgent need for policy makers and service providers to consider the importance of how race, ethnicity, class, gender, sexuality, immigration status, and other identities intersect for Asian Americans rather than treating them each as a static independent category. The model minority stereotype ends up harming Asian American students and families, especially those who need the support. In addition to acknowledging the diversity of Asian Americans, educators and activist scholars must challenge and dismantle damaging and deficit assumptions about Asian Americans, since this population is the fastest growing racial group in the United States. A youth explains the importance of a holistic approach when working with students and their families:

> CBOs know more about the school than the other way around [i.e., schools to CBOs]. My counselors and teachers at school may know what I do, but they don't know what I am struggling with or what I am passionate about. On the other hand, the CYC staffs know what I am struggling with, what I need help with, and what I am passionate about. I think more efforts can be put on the teachers to understand what the students are struggling with outside of school and what the organizations can offer.

In other words, the need to develop *and* maintain relationships is critical. Duncan-Andrade (2007) reminds us "Great teaching will always be about relationships and programs do not build relationships, people do" (p. 636). Essentially, establishing and maintaining strong(er) school, family, and community partnerships should be the purpose where access to information is fluid and transparent for our minoritized communities.

This research has sought to broaden the current and narrow home–school relationship paradigm by including the community, as represented by CBOs, as another pivotal player in the discussion. Implementing and retaining culturally relevant out-of-school time (OST) spaces can assist in strengthening the partnerships between families, communities, and schools. We also need more collaborative research, practices, and policies between family–community–school in order to better serve our students. Accordingly, I make the following recommendations:

For policy makers

- Provide additional and continual funding opportunities for CBOs and other OST spaces to maintain their work and where necessary expand to meet the growing need.

An increase in resources during OST would better serve our children and youth since they spend only 20 percent of their time in school (Miller, 2003). For instance, providing funding to those that encourage and practice culturally relevant family–community–school partnerships.

- Community and youth workers have much to offer to our educational systems.

It is essential to include them in educational dialogue, especially since there is often miscommunication and misconception between schools and communities. In doing so this is when a true partnership between families–communities–schools may take place.

- Listen to the voices that are affected by gentrification and urban renewal.

Listen to understand, rather than listen to respond is necessary. Policy makers and corporations must commit to revitalization of neighborhoods and communities. For instance, revitalization comes from the bottom-up with the community. As a result, housing remains affordable for low-income and working-class people while the neighborhood is improved and upgraded for everyone. Tommy shared what has been happening in Harborview for the past decade:

> They keep building the luxury condos. There's a lot of traffic in Chinatown now. Chinatown is getting torn apart. The high-rises are being built. In 10 years, I don't think you will see small buildings in Chinatown. They will tear everything down.

Michelle similarly expressed, "They are destroying our community!"

For education advocates and school personnel

- Understand that no single entity (e.g., family, school, or community) can improve our educational system alone; instead work to ensure that a dialogical and collaborative approach, which also includes the voices of our children and youth, is implemented in order to better serve them.
- Acknowledge the community as a rich resource and a place of learning *and* teaching.

Recognize CBOs have much to offer to our educational systems and can play an important role in the broad effort to educate our children and youth. Their capacity to develop and maintain culturally relevant and culturally competent services is often in stark contrast to many of our schools. Support their community-based educational workshops and programs that inform minoritized families about the United States and U.S. schools, bridge cultural and generational differences within families, and provide a space for middle and high school Asian American youth during OST.

- Implement policies and procedures that encourage and allow family–community–school partnerships to occur and where a continual and effective agenda is maintained between all groups.

As other scholars have suggested, we need to start "blurring school and community boundaries" (Irby, Pittman, & Tolman, 2003). In doing so, school and community programs are able to support and utilize each other as a resource and each other's work would be enhanced. For instance, implement a local and national network for school personnel and youth and community workers. Rather than viewing the school and community as two separate worlds, immigrant families are then able to feel a sense of unity with the institutions that serve their children.

- Create opportunities for partnerships between higher education, school districts, and CBOs.

In doing so, the relationships between schools and communities are more cooperative and transparent, rather than working on assumptions, hierarchical order, and competitiveness. For instance, support policies and practices that bring together researchers, teacher educators, school personnel, and youth workers. Or schools and CBOs can work together in sponsoring workshops for the community, like the ones at HCCC.

In the case of schools, one way to address and acknowledge the experiences of Asian Americans is infusing Asian American Studies and Ethnic Studies into the K-16 curriculum and culture where students, both Asian Americans and non-Asian Americans, are able to learn about the rich experiences of Asians in the United States. For instance, Samantha noted, "A lot of schools don't have anything related to racism and classes about your own culture and where you came from. So they don't have any of those classes. I feel like those are necessary for everyone." Through implementing an Asian American Studies and Ethnic Studies curriculum, both Students of Color and White students begin to dismantle assumptions. They become critical analyzers in a racialized patriarchal system. Yet, as I will show below, implementing such curriculum is a constant struggle, especially with the high-stakes testing structure in our public schools and a curriculum that does not account for all students' experiences.

The educational leader's role is extremely important here. I recall students and educators in my graduate-level teacher education courses have noted numerous times that multicultural and social justice education are "great" but "what do you do when your principal and administrators are not supportive" or "how are you going to get tenure if you include multicultural education topics that are not covered in the curriculum?" Therefore, educational leaders need to create and maintain institutional capacity for school personnel to do this kind of work. Educational leaders need to be a community liaison. They are the facilitators and supporters in order to build and maintain stronger partnerships with minoritized communities and families. Encouraging and providing opportunities for their school personnel to do justice work is important as well. The educational leaders are bringing the different voices (i.e., students, families/caretakers, school personnel, and communities) together in order to better serve the students.

- It is also crucial that school educators provide a space for their students to embrace their community and culture throughout the year.

Instead of designating the various history months or diversity week celebrations, educators need to incorporate multicultural and social justice education as part of the core curriculum. Students should not be viewed as deficient simply because they are low-income, multilingual, LGBTQ+, and gender nonconforming, or because their families do not speak English. School should be a part of the community; thus students need schools to align with their family and community rather than having these worlds separated. For instance, students should have the opportunity to connect what they are learning in OST educational spaces with their school curriculum. Or invite community members to the classrooms and school as part of a lesson(s) or coteaching a unit(s) that is ongoing. Equally important, policy makers and institutions need to recognize the role and impact that CBOs can play to educate our youth and their communities. Additionally, an increase in resources, support, and collaboration is necessary.

For researchers and scholars

- Further research is needed to include other CBOs and OST spaces and that examine different identities and contexts (e.g., race, ethnicity, social class, sexual orientation, gender, age, language, region, etc.). Comparative and longitudinal studies of different OST spaces would capture these identities and contexts.

- *All* research should honor and work to benefit the community, particularly communities of color that are often marginalized or invisible in academia and the dominant society.

Recognize the dangers of utilizing the term "giving voice" in policy, practice, and research, because it assumes that the "oppressed" (Freire, 1999) do not have a voice and, thus, they must be given permission by an authority (e.g., a researcher) to speak. If researchers are holding to such a belief and mentality then we, too, are guilty of perpetuating oppressive ideology and practices. Rather than giving voice, I "amplify" (Diniz-Pereira, 2005) the voices (i.e., the individuals and communities I collaborate with) that are too often unheard, marginalized, and ignored by the systems and structures that hold inequality in place (for more details, please see Wong, 2008, 2010, 2011, 2013). Furthermore, critical self-reflexivity and humility are extremely crucial practices and processes. Thus, it is important for students to include critical self-reflection early on in their careers and coursework. In other words, self-reflection on privilege, implicit biases, and "capital" is a key aspect of both undergraduate and graduate programs or else, the dominant hierarchical structures perpetuate in a constant oppressive cycle (Wong, 2017).

Additionally, I illustrated the significance of community cultural wealth as a methodological framework to enact justice and equity. As I have expressed, "I have tried my best to amplify and centralize the voices of my collaborators. I suggest all such research should similarly honor and work to benefit the community, particularly communities of color that are often marginalized or invisible in academia and the dominant society" (Wong, 2008, p. 199). As educators, activist scholars, and allies, we have a responsibility to work with and for the people as well as amplify their voices. Moreover, understanding and acknowledging the importance of the community is equally central. For example, HCCC programs all evolved out of the needs of the community, which I noted in the book. Professional development is another important factor that makes HCCC successful. As the Executive Director of HCCC, Susan made it a priority for all of her staff members to have the support and opportunity to attend trainings in their fields. She explained in detail:

> As an agency, and I personally do this, is to encourage staffs to do trainings, to go outside, to talk to other people, to take a full day and do that workshop and we'll pay for it. I want my staff to grow, that's one of my passions because you should always grow your staff, whether they stay with your agency or leave. For instance, making sure your staffs have opportunities to keep learning and keep applying what they learned and to keep them at the top of their game. And to give them opportunities to learn more, to develop their own skills, and to find and hone the skills that they do have, so that there's room for growth. You give them the support that they need. You give them the workshops and trainings that they need to go to. You build it into their day.

You know, make it a part of what they do. There are some agencies, in order to cut cost, won't put any money into staff training or funding for workshops because it's a waste of money. But in the end, you end up losing as an agency, because your staffs stagnate if they don't get any new ideas, if they don't keep track of the trends in your field because the policy changes.

Moreover, in order to build and maintain a strong presence in the community, providing a space for staffs to grow is critical. Whether this means providing opportunities to grow within the organization or apply your skills elsewhere because, as one of the HCCC staff expressed, "It's really about working for the community." Susan also noted a key component to community work is serving the people:

> I believe that people, who do community service work, direct services work, and nonprofit work, the benefit is not just for your own agency, but it's for your larger community. If HCCC can be the grooming ground for people to start their own agencies or for people to start their own programming—great, go do it, because there are not enough valuable services.

In doing so, the community recognizes the quality and commitment of HCCC. As I have illustrated throughout this book, the young people and their parents clearly noticed a difference between the services at HCCC and other OST educational spaces in the area. For example, a high school youth explained her reasons for coming to CYC: "It's just a place to be ... you can be yourself here. You don't get that [feeling] elsewhere."

Considerations for future research

The OST literature noted that parents and schools cannot be the only ones who are "doing it all," and thus CBOs are a great resource in bridging the family, school, and community (McLaughlin & Heath, 1994; McLaughlin, Irby, & Langman, 1994; Piha & Adams, 2001). McLaughlin and Heath (1994) assert:

> Youth organizations can provide a bridge to mainstream institutions for both students and their parents; they can furnish schools with important knowledge about youth and their families. They can furnish families with information, access, and opportunities to play a positive role in youth's development ... Together, schools and CBOs can create multiple opportunities for learning and enhance the diversity of experience available to young people. (p. 295)

However, it is also important to note that CBOs can not do it all; rather, a holistic and collaborative approach should be implemented in which partnerships are created and maintained in our communities with the mutual goal of improved service to our students through more effective communication and understanding of the unique needs of students of color from immigrant families. Equally important, policy makers need to recognize the role that CBOs can play in the broad effort to educate our youth, and to recognize the importance of funding CBOs to maintain their work and where necessary expand to meet growing need. An increase in resources might create opportunities for collaboration and growth in CBOs that can positively impact the youth, their families, and their community.

CBOs have much to offer to our educational systems as well. Their capacity to develop and maintain culturally relevant programs is in stark contrast to the lack of many of our schools to do the same. In order to better serve our youth, teacher education programs also should collaborate with OST spaces and youth workers. For instance, I have organized a panel of youth and community workers to come to my graduate-level teacher education class and share some of their experiences working with youth and their communities during the OST and to bring awareness of the different community resources that are available. In doing so, school personnel and community workers were able to form partnerships. Afterward, my students expressed the importance of such a panel discussion: "the panel served as an eye-opening and enlightening experience" particularly since "youth and community work are never talked about in the schools and in our classes." More importantly, with the increase in standard-based reforms across the nation today, CBOs are a way to bridge families and schools. Thus, schools, families, and CBOs need to form strong(er) partnerships where a continual and effective agenda is maintained between all of the groups. When schools build and maintain strong relationships with CBOs, they are better positioned to understand the lives of their students, families, and communities that they serve. At the same time, it is necessary but insufficient to merely understand the lives of our students. Understanding must lead to well-conceived action. The social capital necessary to negotiate our structures of education should be interrogated and made transparent. As other scholars have noted (Irby et al., 2003; McLaughlin & Heath, 1994; McLaughlin et al., 1994; Noam, 2003), we need to start "blurring school and community boundaries" (Irby et al., 2003). In doing so, both the school and out-of-school educational spaces are able to see each other as a resource. Rather than viewing the school and community as two separate worlds, parents and families are then able to feel a sense of unity with the two institutions that serve their children and family. CBOs can play a crucial role in this transformation.

Additionally, this research illuminated OST educational spaces and CBOs through detailed portraits and an educational lens. It also examined the educational, social and emotional, and leadership services and support for Chinese

American youth from low-income immigrant families, a group that has been labeled as the "model minority." This book, however, focused on one OST space and CBO. As a result, further research is needed to include other CBOs and OST educational spaces. That being said, a comparative and longitudinal study of different OST spaces would capture what are some similarities and differences. Moreover, through more detailed research of OST educational spaces, other institutions (e.g., schools and funding agencies) could build greater collaborations. There are still countless portraits and stories that have not been captured and amplified; and thus there remains a much needed research on CBOs.

In 2014, for the first time, over fifty percent in U.S. public schools are students of color. Moreover, as the children of the immigrant population are increasing in our schools, educators need to understand both the cultural and social dynamics of their students. However, only eighteen percent of our teachers are teachers of color, thus are not demographically reflective of the students they serve. The racial disparity between U.S. public school teachers and their students prompts the need to examine how teacher education programs recruit and retain teacher candidates of color and how school districts are supporting and retaining their educators.

One approach schools have addressed their diverse student population is establishing ethnic clubs. However, having "Asian American Clubs" in the schools is ineffective if the clubs are being marginalized from the rest of the school. Or even highly acknowledging the school's long-standing academic excellence and the diversity of the student population is simply ignoring the "real" issues in schools today. I find Ogletree, Bell, and Smith's (2002) statement extremely relevant in which they discuss our nation's approach in serving youth:

> The nation's current approach to the needs of young people is reactive, problem focused, fragmented, and incomplete. It may guarantee every youth a prison cell, but it cannot guarantee them an after-school program, job opportunity, or safe environment. Its programs fall short in quantity, quality, duration, and outreach to those most in need. (p. 41)

Educators and policy makers should view our youth as assets instead of the problem and deficit. In doing so, the voices of young people should be a part of the dialogue.

As educators, community organizers, and activist scholars, we need to believe that *every* student, who enters our educational settings and lives, is able to succeed. I am ending this book with a quote by bell hooks (2003) to remind us as activist scholars and educators that "hope" for learning is transformative:

My hope emerges from those places of struggle where I witness individuals positively transforming their lives and the world around them. Educating is always a vocation rooted in hopefulness. As teachers we believe that learning is possible, that nothing can keep an open mind from seeking after knowledge and finding a way to know. (p. xiv)

Works cited

Diniz-Pereira, J. E. (2005). *"How the dreamers are born" The identity construction of activist educators: Life histories of women educators from the Landless Workers Movement in Brazil* (Doctoral dissertation). Department of Curriculum and Instruction, University of Wisconsin-Madison.

Duncan-Andrade, J. (2007). Gangstas, Wankstas, and Ridas: Defining, developing, and supporting effective teachers in urban schools. *International Journal of Qualitative Studies in Education, 20*(6), 617–638.

Freire, P. (1999). *Pedagogy of the oppressed.* New York, NY: The Continuum Publishing.

hooks, b. (2003). *Teaching community: A pedagogy of hope.* New York, NY: Routledge.

Irby, M., Pittman, K. J., & Tolman, J. (2003, Spring). Blurring the lines: Expanding learning opportunities for children and youth. In M. Irby, K. J. Pittman, & J. Tolman (Eds.), *When, where, what and how youth learn: Blurring school and community boundaries* (pp. 13–28). New Directions for Youth Development: Theory Practice Research, No. 97. San Francisco, CA: Jossey-Bass.

McLaughlin, M. W., & Heath, S. B. (1994, August). The best of both worlds: Connecting schools and community youth organizations for all-day, all-year learning. *Educational Administration Quarterly, 30*(3), 278–300.

McLaughlin, M. W., Irby, M. A., & Langman, J. (1994). *Urban sanctuaries: Neighborhood organizations in the lives and future of inner-city youth.* San Francisco, CA: Jossey-Bass.

Miller, B. M. (2003). *Critical Hours: Afterschool Programs and Educational Success.* Quincy, MA: Nellie Mae Education Foundation.

Noam, G. G. (2003, Spring). Learning with excitement: Bridging school and after-school worlds and project-based learning. In M. Irby, K. J. Pittman, & J. Tolman (Eds.), *When, where, what and how youth learn: Blurring school and community boundaries* (pp. 121–138). New Directions for Youth Development: Theory Practice Research, No. 97. San Francisco, CA: Jossey-Bass.

Ogletree, R., Bell, T., & Smith, N. K. (2002, Summer). Positive youth development initiatives in Chicago. In G. G. Noam & B. M. Miller (Eds.), *Youth development and after-school time: A tale of many cities* (pp. 41–64). New Directions for Youth Development: Theory Practice Research, No. 94. San Francisco, CA: Jossey-Bass.

Piha, S., & Adams, A. (2001). *Youth development guide: Engaging young people in after-school programming.* San Francisco, CA: Community Network for Youth Development.

Wong, N. W. A. (2008). "They see us as resource": The role of a community-based youth center in supporting the academic lives of low-income Chinese American Youth. *Anthropology & Education Quarterly, 39*(2), 181–204.

Wong, N. W. A. (2010). "Cuz they care about the people who goes there": The multiple roles of a community-based youth center in providing "Youth (Comm)Unity" for low-income Chinese American youth. *Urban Education, 45*(5), 708–739.

Wong, N. W. A. (2011). Broadening support for Asian American and Pacific Islander immigrant families: The role and impact of community-based organizations in family-community-school partnerships. *AAPI Nexus: Policy, Practice and Community, 9*(1–2), 134–142.

Wong, N. W. A. (2013). "Like a bridge": How a community-based organization helps immigrant and working poor Chinese parents navigate U.S. schools. In R. Endo & X. L. Rong (Eds.), *Educating Asian Americans: Achievement, schooling, and identities* (pp. 181–204). Charlotte, NC: Information Age Publishing.

Wong, N. W. A. (2017). "Lovely to me": An immigrant's daughter's critical self-reflexivity research journey. *Journal of Critical Thought and Praxis, 6*(2), 84–94.

Index

sj Miller & Leslie David Burns
GENERAL EDITORS

Social Justice Across Contexts in Education addresses how teaching for social justice, broadly defined, mediates and disrupts systemic and structural inequities across early childhood, K–12 and postsecondary disciplinary, interdisciplinary and/or trans-disciplinary educational contexts. This series includes books exploring how theory informs sustainable pedagogies for social justice curriculum and instruction, and how research, methodology, and assessment can inform equitable and responsive teaching. The series constructs, advances, and supports socially just policies and practices for all individuals and groups across the spectrum of our society's education system.

Books in this series provide sustainable models for generating theories, research, practices, and tools for social justice across contexts as a means to leverage the psychological, emotional, and cognitive growth for learners and professionals. They position social justice as a fundamental aspect of schooling, and prepare readers to advocate for and prevent social justice from becoming marginalized by reform movements in favor of the corporatization and de-professionalization of education. The over-arching aim is to establish a true field of social justice education that offers theory, knowledge, and resources for those who seek to help all learners succeed. It speaks for, about, and to classroom teachers, administrators, teacher educators, education researchers, students, and other key constituents who are committed to transforming the landscape of schools and communities.

Send proposals and manuscripts to the general editors at:

sj Miller   sj.Miller@colorado.edu
Leslie David Burns   L.Burns@uky.edu

To order other books in this series, please contact our Customer Service Department at:

(800) 770-LANG (within the U.S.)
(212) 647-7706 (outside the U.S.)
(212) 647-7707 FAX

or browse online by series at:

WWW.PETERLANG.COM

CPSIA information can be obtained
at www.ICGtesting.com
Printed in the USA
LVHW081754230623
750622LV00006B/195

9 781433 146855